Mastering
iPhone 15
Camera

Beginners to Professional Guide to Digital Photography, Videography and Storytelling using iPhone 15 Camera

Fritsche King

Copyright © 2023 **Fritsche King**

All Rights Reserved

This book or parts thereof may not be reproduced in any form, stored in any retrieval system, or transmitted in any form by any means—electronic, mechanical, photocopy, recording, or otherwise—without prior written permission of the publisher, except as provided by United States of America copyright law and fair use.

Disclaimer and Terms of Use

The author and publisher of this book and the accompanying materials have used their best efforts in preparing this book. The author and publisher make no representation or warranties with respect to the accuracy, applicability, fitness, or completeness of the contents of this book. The information contained in this book is strictly for informational purposes. Therefore, if you wish to apply the ideas contained in this book, you are taking full responsibility for your actions.

Printed in the United States of America

TABLE OF CONTENTS

TABLE OF CONTENTS III

INTRODUCTION 1

CHAPTER ONE 3

GETTING STARTED 3

   OVERVIEW 3
   NEW CAMERA FEATURES IN IPHONE 15 SERIES 3
      IPhone 15 and iPhone 15 Plus 3
      IPhone 15 Pro and iPhone 15 Pro Max 5
   HOW TO OPEN THE CAMERA 6
   HOW TO MASTER THE CAMERA APP 8
      How to master the camera app on iPhone 15 Pro — Physical buttons................... 8
      How to master the camera app on iPhone 15 - On-screen controls 11
      Zoom levels on iPhone 15 Pro and iPhone 15 Pro Max 12
      How to master the camera app on iPhone 15 - Additional controls and settings.... 13
      How to master the camera app on iPhone 15 - Extra shooting modes 14
   VIDEO ON IPHONE 15 PRO AND IPHONE 15 PRO MAX 16
      How to master the camera app on iPhone 15 pro - Other settings 17
   HOW TO TAKE A PICTURE OR RECORD A VIDEO 17
      Take a photo 17
      Record videos with your iPhone camera 17
      Record a Video 18
      Record HD or 4K video 18
   HOW TO SHOOT VIDEO ON AN IPHONE: RECORD PROFESSIONAL VIDEOS 18
   TAKE PANORAMIC PHOTOS WITH YOUR IPHONE CAMERA 21
   HOW TO TAKE PHOTOS FROM A VIDEO 21
   CAPTURE A STILL IMAGE FROM A VIDEO ON AN IPHONE 22
   HOW TO CHANGE THE CAMERA MODES 22
   HOW TO CAPTURE LOG FOOTAGE ON AN IPHONE 15 PRO VERSIONS 23
   HOW TO ZOOM IN AND ZOOM OUT 26
   HOW TO ADJUST THE SHUTTER VOLUME 26
      Simple Methods to Turn Off Camera Sound 26
      Turn on Silent Mode 26
      Enable Live Photos 27
   REDUCE THE VOLUME OF YOUR IPHONE UNDER THE CONTROL CENTER 27
      While the music is playing, take photos or screenshots 28
      While recording videos, take photos or screenshots 28
   HOW TO CHANGE THE HDR CAMERA SETTINGS 28
      Changing the HDR camera settings 28
      Disable automatic HDR 29

Turn off and on HDR video 29
How to customize the main camera lens 29
Top 5 iPhone Camera Settings for Better Video Quality 30
Lighting 32
Composition 32
Better Exposure 33
White Balance 33
Frequently Asked Questions 33

CHAPTER TWO 34

VIDEO RECORDING 34

Overview 34
How to record a QuickTake video 34
How to Use QuickTake for Taking Burst 35
Shoot QuickTake with the volume up button 35
How to record a time-lapse video 35
Experiment with Time-Lapse in Night Mode 37
Change the camera's video recording settings on iPhone 37
Change the Auto FPS settings 37
Turn on and off the stereo recording 38
Turn off and on HDR video 38
Turn Lock Camera on and off 38
Turn on and off Enhanced Stabilization 38
Turn on and off Lock White Balance 38
How to Change iPhone Time Lapse Settings 39
Tips to make a perfect Time-lapse video on iPhone 39
How to record a slow-motion video 40
How slow motion works on iPhone 40
What is the speed of an iPhone slow-motion video? 40
Shooting slow motion using an iPhone camera 40
How to Change iPhone Slo-mo Settings 40
How to shoot a slow-motion video with your iPhone 42
How to Make Your Slow Motion Video Pop 42
How to convert normal video to slo-mo 42
How to speed up a slow-motion video 44
How to slow down your video 45
How to trim, crop, and straighten your slow-motion video 45
How to adjust exposure, contrast, and color for a Slo-mo video 46
How to use action mode 47
How to customize Action Mode 49
Frequently Asked Questions 50

CHAPTER THREE 51

RECORDING IN PRORAW AND PRORES 51
   OVERVIEW 51
   HOW TO RECORD IN PRORAW AND PRORES ON THE IPHONE 15 PRO AND 15 PRO MAX 51
      The Benefits of Using ProRAW and ProRes 51
      Disadvantages of using ProRAW and ProRes 51
      How much space are ProRAW and ProRes capture going to take up? 52
   HOW TO CAPTURE IN PRORAW 52
      Turn on Apple ProRAW 52
   TAKE RAW PICTURES 53
   HOW TO RECORD IN PRORES ON IPHONE 15 SERIES 54
      Enable ProRes 54
      Record in ProRes 55
   TOP IPHONE 15 PRO & MAX ACCESSORIES FOR FILMMAKING 57
   RODE VIDEOMIC ME COMPACT TRRS CARDIOID MICROPHONE FOR IPHONE 58
   HOW TO REMOVE OBJECTS IN PHOTOS 63
      Remove the Object 63
      In contrast to the original 63
   HOW TO RECORD CINEMATIC VIDEO 64
   HOW TO SHOOT VIDEOS IN CINEMATIC MODE 64
   HOW TO ADJUST CINEMATIC MODE FOCUS POST-SHOOT 65
   HOW TO TRIM A VIDEO 67
      Trimming a Video in the Photos App 67
      Trimming an iPhone video for Instagram 69
   HOW TO CUT A VIDEO ON IPHONE INTO PARTS 69
      How to Use iMovie to Split and Rearrange Clips 69
      How to cut a clip out of a video 70
   HOW TO RECORD THE SCREEN 71
      Add the screen recorder to the control center 71
      Customize the Recording Audio Settings (Optional) 72
      End the Recording 72
   FREQUENTLY ASKED QUESTIONS 72

CHAPTER FOUR 73

PHOTOGRAPHIC STYLES, EXPOSURE, AND OTHER CAMERA SETTINGS 73
   OVERVIEW 73
   WHAT EXACTLY ARE PHOTOGRAPHIC STYLES? 73
      Why are photographic styles so appealing? 73
   HOW TO SET UP PHOTOGRAPHIC STYLES 74
      Create a standard photographic style 74
      Create a Photographic Style in the Camera app 74
   HOW TO TURN THE CAMERA FLASH ON OR OFF 75
   HOW TO ADJUST FOCUS AND EXPOSURE 75

How to use a timer 77
How can I disable the timer on my iPhone 15 camera? 79
    How does the iPhone camera timer work? 79
    Tips for Using the Timer on an iPhone to Take Photos 79
How to set a timer on iPhone 15 without Burst? 80
How to take a photo with a filter 80
    How to use the iPhone camera app to capture a shot with a filter 81
    How to add a filter to a photo you've already taken 81
    Default photo filters and how they transform photos 81
How to align your photo using a grid 82
Using the Rule of Thirds in Your iPhone Photos 83
Frequently Asked Questions 84

CHAPTER FIVE 85

PHOTOS APP 85

Overview 85
How to navigate through the Photos app 85
    View photos and videos in the Photos app on the iPhone 85
    How photos and videos are organized in Photos 85
    Browse photos in your library 86
    View individual images 86
    See photo and video information 86
How to Delete and Share Photos 87
    Delete 87
Share 89
    Share photos and videos on iPhone 89
    Adjust the sharing options 91
    Share photos and videos by bringing one iPhone close to another 91
    Save or share a photo or video you receive 92
Import and Export Videos 92
    Import and export photos and videos on iPhone 92
    Import photos and videos to your iPhone 92
Export photos and videos to an external storage device 93
Share long videos on your iPhone 94
    Use AirDrop to send a video 94
    Send a video using an iCloud link 94
    Send a video using Mail Drop 94
How to add text to your pictures 95
    Using Apple's Photos app 95
    Using Phonto 96
How to Recover Deleted Pictures and Videos from the Photos App 97
    Is it possible to restore lost images from an iPhone 15? 98
How to make a photo part of your favorite 100

How to hide photos and videos and access them 102
    How to unhide or view hidden photos 103
How to crop, flip, and rotate photos 104
    Cropping photos 104
    Flipping Photos 104
    Rotating Photos 104
How to change the lighting and color scheme 105
    Adjust the screen brightness and color on the iPhone 105
    Manually adjust the screen brightness 105
    Automatically adjust the screen brightness 105
    Turn Dark Mode on or off 105
Schedule Dark Mode to turn on and off automatically 106
    Turn the Night Shift on or off 107
    Schedule the Night Shift to turn on and off automatically 107
    Turn True Tone on or off 107
How to revert an adjusted image 108
Frequently Asked Questions 109

CHAPTER SIX 110

FACETIME 110

Overview 110
How to set up FaceTime 110
    Log in with your Apple ID 110
    Turn on FaceTime 110
    Open FaceTime 111
How to make and receive a FaceTime call 111
Make a FaceTime Call 111
    Receive a FaceTime Call 112
    Record a video message 112
Leave a voicemail 113
    Call again 113
    During a FaceTime call 113
How to use Memoji on FaceTime 113
How to start a FaceTime Audio/Video call from messages 115
How to create a link to a FaceTime call 115
How to turn on live captions for FaceTime calls 116
How to include background sounds on a FaceTime call 116
How to share your screen on a FaceTime call 117
How to blur the background using portrait mode 117
Take a Live Photo in FaceTime on an iPhone 118
Frequently Asked Questions 118

CHAPTER SEVEN 119

MEMORY MOVIES 119
   OVERVIEW 119
   HOW TO CREATE A MEMORY MOVIE 119
      What exactly are iPhone Memories? 119
      Editing Pre-Made iPhone Memories 119
      How to share your favorite memories 121
      How to change the memory mix 121
   MANUALLY CREATING A MEMORY ON YOUR IPHONE 123
      Creating a Memory from an Album or Day/ Month 124
      Creating a Memory for a Person 125
   EDITING A MEMORY 126
      Changing the Title 127
   HOW TO ADD AND REMOVE PHOTOS WITHIN MEMORY 127
   ADJUST THE LENGTH 128
      Protect the Memories Video 129
   BACKUP IPHONE MEMORY VIDEOS USING ICLOUD 129
   HOW TO CREATE NEW ALBUMS IN THE PHOTOS APP 130
      What Is the Difference Between an iPhone Folder and a Photo Album? 130
      How to Create an Album in Photos 130
   HOW TO CREATE A FOLDER IN PHOTOS 132
   HOW TO ADD AN ALBUM TO A FOLDER 133
      How to Move an Existing Album into a Folder on iPhone 134
   HOW TO CHANGE A PHOTO ALBUM'S COVER PHOTO 135
      How to Change the Cover Photo of an Album in Photos 135
   HOW TO DELETE UNNECESSARY PHOTO ALBUMS 136
   HOW TO ORGANIZE PHOTOS IN AN ALBUM 137
   HOW TO IDENTIFY AND REMOVE IDENTICAL-LOOKING IMAGES 138
   HOW TO DELETE BURST PHOTOS 138
   IS IT BAD THAT I HAVE SO MANY DUPLICATES? 139
   HOW TO RENAME PHOTOS ON IPHONE 140
      How to quickly rename iPhone Screenshots 140
      Renaming Photos on iPhone 141
      Change how photos appear in an album 141
   FREQUENTLY ASKED QUESTIONS 142

CHAPTER EIGHT 143

MACRO PHOTOGRAPHY AND OTHER CAMERA MODES 143
   OVERVIEW 143
   WHAT EXACTLY ARE MACRO PHOTOS? 143
      Which iPhones are capable of macro photography? 143
      How to Shoot Macro Photos on an iPhone 15 Series 143
      How to use automatic macro switching control 144

viii

- *How to shoot macro video in time-lapse or slow-motion* 144
- HOW TO TAKE A PICTURE IN PORTRAIT MODE 145
  - *How to Turn Photos into Portraits after Shooting* 145
- QUICKLY CONVERT A PHOTO TO A PORTRAIT 146
  - *Edit the Portrait Effect in Photos* 146
  - *Turn off Auto Portrait Capture* 147
- ADJUST DEPTH CONTROL AND PORTRAIT LIGHTING 147
- REMOVE THE PORTRAIT MODE EFFECT 148
  - *How to take a picture in night mode* 148
  - *How Does Night Mode Function?* 148
  - *Which iPhones have night mode?* 149
  - *How to Use Night Mode* 149
  - *Change the capture time* 149
- TIPS FOR BETTER NIGHT PHOTOGRAPHY 149
- HOW TO USE LIVE TEXT WITH THE CAMERA 150
  - *The benefit of Live Text?* 150
  - *IPhone Photos: How to Use Live Text* 150
  - *How to Use Live Text in the Camera on iPhone* 152
- HOW TO USE DEPTH CONTROL 153
  - *Before Taking a Photo* 153
  - *After Taking a Photo* 153
- HOW TO UPLOAD YOUR PHOTOS AND KEEP THEM SAFE 154
  - *Use iCloud Photos* 154
  - *How to Enable iCloud Photos* 154
  - *Increase iPhone Storage* 154
  - *Backup to iCloud* 154
  - *Enable iCloud Backup* 154
  - *Use My Photo Stream* 155
  - *Enable My Photo Stream* 155
  - *Use AirDrop* 155
  - *Save Photos to Files* 155
  - *Use third-party cloud services* 155
- ORGANIZE AND DELETE UNWANTED PHOTOS REGULARLY 155
  - *Use Password Security and Biometrics* 156
  - *Enable two-factor authentication* 156
  - *Use a VPN for Additional Security* 156
  - *Backup your photos locally* 156
- HOW TO SCAN QR CODES 156
- FREQUENTLY ASKED QUESTIONS 158

CHAPTER NINE 159

TROUBLESHOOTING ISSUES 159

- OVERVIEW 159

How to Solve Camera Crashes 159
   Restart your iPhone *159*
   Close Background Apps *159*
   Update iOS *159*
   Reset Camera Settings *159*
   Clear Camera Cache *160*
   Free Up Storage Space *160*
   Examine Third-Party Camera Apps *160*
   Reset All Settings *160*
   Perform a Factory Reset *160*
   Contact Apple Support *160*
How to troubleshoot iPhone 15 Series Blurry Photos and Videos 160
The Most Common Causes of Blurry Photos and Videos 161
Camera Tips 161
   Change the Camera Settings *161*
   Enable Apple ProRAW *161*
   Prepare Phone Storage *162*
   Choose your Style *162*
   Preserve Settings *162*
Use Macro Control 162
   Use Shutter Button *163*
   Take a Burst *163*
   Change Exposure *163*
Consider Dynamic Island 163
   Use Live Photo *164*
   Include Filters *164*
   Auto Edit *164*
   Custom Edit *164*
Troubleshooting For Sharper Photos 165
   Enable QuickTake Video Stabilization *165*
Change the Camera Settings 165
Set the Focus 166
   Use Night Mode *167*
Avoid using Digital Zoom 168
   Use a tripod to keep your phone steady *168*
   Clean the Lens of the Rear Camera *168*
IPhone 15 Camera Not Focusing Issues 169
   Dirty External Lens *169*
   Remove the Case *169*
   Assist your iPhone in focusing *170*
   Restart the Camera app *170*
   Force Restart iPhone *170*
   DFU Restore *170*

- Get Apple Support 171
- HOW TO FIX THE CAMERA FLASH NOT WORKING 171
  - Errors Caused by "iPhone Flash is Disabled" 171
- HOW TO REPAIR AN IPHONE FLASHLIGHT THAT ISN'T WORKING 172
  - Close the Camera application 173
  - Charge your iPhone first 173
  - Remove the iPhone Cover if Covered 173
  - Turn the Camera flash ON and then OFF 173
  - Restart your iPhone 173
  - Check and Install Updates 173
  - Reset iPhone Settings 174
  - Force Restart iPhone 174
  - Toggle Low Power Mode on and off 174
  - Optimize battery charging by turning on and off 175
- HOW TO FIX A NON-WORKING CAMERA 175
- HOW TO TROUBLESHOOT NIGHT MODE ISSUES 175
  - Ensure that your software is up to date 175
  - Examine the Camera Settings 175
  - Stable Support 176
  - Clean the Lens of the Camera 176
  - Avoid Using Extremely Low Lighting 176
  - Experiment with Exposure Time 176
  - Use a Flash 176
  - Composition and Focus 176
  - Take Multiple Photos 176
  - Reboot your iPhone 177
  - Examine for Hardware Issues 177
  - Speak with Apple Support 177
- HOW TO CORRECT INCONSISTENT PORTRAIT MODE 177
  - Clean the Camera Lens 177
  - Provide Adequate Lighting 177
  - iOS Update 177
  - Reset Camera Settings 178
  - Adjust the focus and exposure 178
  - Adjust the Depth Control 178
  - Examine for Conflicting Objects 178
  - Maintain the Proper Distance 178
  - Avoid cluttered backgrounds 178
  - Experiment with Lighting Effects 178
  - Use a tripod or other kind of stabilization 178
  - Take Several Shots 179
  - Use Third-Party Apps 179
  - Get in touch with Apple Support 179

How to solve live photos not playing 179
    Check that Live Photos is enabled 179
    Examine Storage Space 179
    Examine the Camera Settings 179
    Reboot your iPhone 180
    Update iOS 180
    Force Restart 180
    Reset All Settings 180
    Restoring from Backup 180
    Get in touch with Apple Support 180
IPhone Continuity Camera Isn't Working 181
    What exactly is a Continuity Camera? 181
    How to Repair Chrome's Continuity Camera 181
Frequently Asked Questions 182
CONCLUSION 182

INDEX **184**

INTRODUCTION

Ladies and gentlemen, tech enthusiasts and photography aficionados, welcome to the dawn of a new era in smartphone photography – the iPhone 15 Series. Apple's latest flagship devices have arrived, and they're armed to the teeth with groundbreaking camera innovations that are bound to ignite your creativity and redefine your photography experience. So, grab your iPhone 15, 15 Plus, 15 Pro, or 15 Pro Max, and let's embark on a thrilling journey through the world of visual storytelling!

Beyond Evolution: The iPhone 15 Pro Camera Experience

Picture this: you're standing on the precipice of a breathtaking landscape, and you reach for your iPhone 15 Pro. As you frame the shot, you're about to capture every exquisite detail, from the smallest dewdrop on a leaf to the grandeur of a sweeping mountain range. The iPhone 15 Pro camera stands as the heart and soul of these devices, and Apple has poured countless hours of engineering prowess into refining this masterpiece.

But what sets the iPhone 15 Pro apart from its predecessors? We're talking about a monumental leap in camera technology. The Pro and Pro Max models boast an awe-inspiring 48MP main camera, ensuring that your images are vivid, sharp, and brimming with lifelike details. With higher resolutions, your photos are destined for the hall of fame, and your memories will be etched in pixel-perfect perfection.

🔍 Zooming into the Future: Lossless Digital Zoom and More

Imagine the excitement of being able to zoom into a scene, capturing intricate details without losing quality. With the iPhone 15 and 15 Plus, you can make use of the lossless digital zoom capabilities that elevate your photography game to new heights. Say goodbye to grainy, distorted zoomed-in photos – Apple's technological wizardry guarantees that every zoomed shot is as crisp as your initial frame.

The 48MP camera in these models isn't just about pixel power; it's a tool for unleashing your creative vision. Whether you're capturing a sweeping vista or a captivating close-up, your iPhone 15 will be your trusty companion, delivering unparalleled image quality with every click.

✹ The Pro Max's Marvel: Unleashing the Power of Telephoto

Hold your breath as we delve into the iPhone 15 Pro Max's pièce de résistance — the upgraded telephoto camera. It's not just an enhancement; it's a revelation. Get ready to explore the world of telephoto photography like never before. With a telephoto camera that boasts enhanced capabilities, you can now zoom in closer to subjects without physically moving, preserving the integrity of your shots.

Whether you're capturing a fleeting moment at a sports event, a mesmerizing portrait, or the intricate architecture of a historic building, the iPhone 15 Pro Max has the tools to make every shot a masterpiece. It's the ultimate fusion of technology and artistry.

🎛 Software Meets Hardware: A Harmonious Blend

The iPhone 15 Series' camera improvements aren't just limited to hardware. Apple has honed the software that drives these incredible lenses, ensuring that your photography experience is seamless and intuitive. From advanced image processing algorithms to innovative shooting modes, you're in control of a camera that adapts to your needs, no matter your skill level.

In this comprehensive iPhone 15 Camera Guide, we'll dive deep into the intricacies of both hardware and software, providing you with expert tips and tricks to elevate your photography game. Whether you're a seasoned pro or a budding photographer, there's something here for everyone.

Stay tuned for a captivating exploration of the iPhone 15 camera features, a closer look at the Pro and Pro Max camera systems, and a treasure trove of creative ideas that will inspire you to push the boundaries of mobile photography. Your iPhone 15 is your canvas, and the world is your muse — let's seize the moment together!

Are you ready to unlock the true potential of your iPhone 15's camera? Let's embark on this thrilling adventure together!

CHAPTER ONE
GETTING STARTED

Overview

Chapter one introduces us to the new features and functions of the iPhone 15 Series camera. Here, you will also get to see how to open the camera app the easy way and how to master the camera app overall.

New Camera Features in iPhone 15 Series

IPhone 15 and iPhone 15 Plus

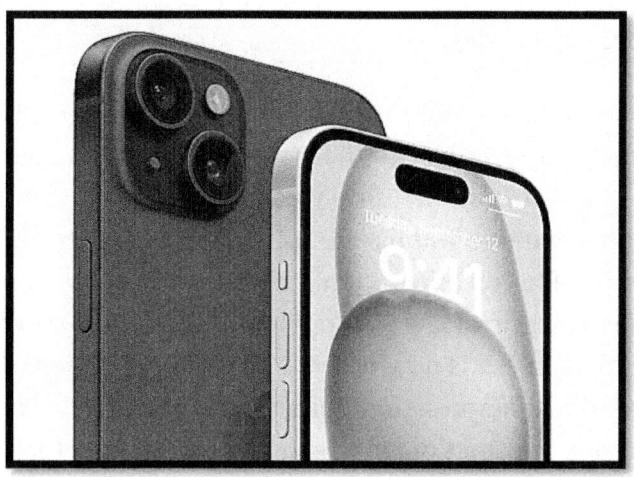

The prominent addition to the iPhone 15 and iPhone 15 Plus is the inclusion of a 48 MP primary camera. The inclusion of a wider aperture and a higher default resolution of 24MP in this device is expected to yield images that are characterized by enhanced brightness, richer color reproduction, and greater levels of detail when compared to those captured by the iPhone 14. This entails capturing photos at a resolution four times higher than that of the previous model, resulting in exceptionally high-resolution images. Additionally, it facilitates capturing shots with a 2x zoom on the telephoto lens while maintaining optimal picture quality. According to Apple, this feature effectively simulates the presence of a third camera. The main camera boasts a focal length of 26mm, an impressive f/1.6 aperture, and features such as sensor-shift optical image stabilization (OIS), among other notable attributes. An intriguing inclusion in Apple's latest offering is the incorporation of a 24MP super-high-resolution camera, complemented by the presence of 48MP photographs that exude exceptional quality.

The iPhone 15 maintains the dual camera setup from the previous year, featuring a secondary lens that is a 12MP Ultra-Wide camera equipped with a 13mm focal length and an f/2.4 aperture. As indicated, Apple additionally promotes the capability of capturing 12MP 2x Telephoto shots facilitated by the quad-pixel sensor as an independent attribute, boasting a focal length of 52mm and an aperture of f/1.6. The iPhone 15 is equipped with Smart HDR 5, which effectively addresses challenges posed by intense or inconsistent lighting conditions. Apple has implemented notable enhancements to the portrait mode feature on the iPhone 15, resulting in an improved user experience characterized by enhanced sharpness, more vibrant color reproduction, and superior low-light performance. Furthermore, portrait mode has undergone a comprehensive overhaul, further augmenting its capabilities.

The Camera app now possesses the capability to autonomously activate Portrait mode upon detecting a compatible subject, similar to the previous functionality of earlier versions of iPhones that would automatically engage macro or night modes. Even in the absence of using portrait mode during the initial capture, it is possible to activate it subsequently within the Photos application. Additionally, one can modify the focus to significantly alter the aesthetic of the photograph in case the desired outcome was not achieved initially. Remarkably, it is now possible to capture portrait photos even without activating the portrait mode feature. Additionally, one can edit photos within the Photos app by using the depth information that is automatically captured during the initial shooting process.

As anticipated, the computational capabilities are driven by the A16 Bionic chip, which was introduced in the previous version of the iPhone, the iPhone 14 pro. This advanced chip plays a crucial role in enhancing the overall performance of the device. Moreso, the iPhone 15 maintains numerous camera functionalities from the previous version, encompassing 4K video capture at a maximum frame rate of 60 frames per second, the inclusion of Cinematic mode, the ability to record HDR videos in 4K at 60 frames per second, and additional features. The device continues to provide users with the convenience of a 12MP front-facing True Depth Camera, enabling them to engage in FaceTime calls, captures stunning selfies, and record high-quality videos.

IPhone 15 Pro and iPhone 15 Pro Max

The iPhone 15 Pro and iPhone 15 Pro Max is equipped with the same 48MP main camera found in their predecessor, the iPhone 14 Pro. The sensor used in the iPhone 15/15 Plus differs from its predecessor, enabling the capability to capture images at both 24MP and 48MP resolutions. This can be achieved through the use of either ProRAW or HEIF formats. The utilization of ProRAW in the iPhone 14 Pro was necessary to fully leverage the device's extensive pixel capabilities. Consequently, Apple has thoughtfully introduced a more condensed format to cater to users seeking to optimize their storage capacity. The enhancements made to the camera of the iPhone 15 Pro were relatively subdued in comparison to previous iterations. The device retains its 48MP camera, allowing for the capture of super-high-resolution shots at 24MP, akin to the capabilities of the iPhone 15. Additionally, it provides support for 48MP HEIF images, enabling users to capture shots with four times the resolution of standard HEIF images, while minimizing storage consumption. According to Apple, the default mode for the rear camera is equipped with a 24mm lens equivalent, which is particularly well-suited for capturing images with a significant sense of depth. If one desires a default camera setting with a greater level of zoom, such as for capturing portrait-style photographs, it is also possible to establish a 28mm or 35mm equivalent focal length. This adjustment facilitates the ability to focus the image on a specific subject. The 48-megapixel camera maintains a 24mm focal length and an aperture of f/1.78. Additionally, the device is equipped with a secondary camera featuring a 12-megapixel ultra-wide lens and a third camera with a 12-megapixel telephoto lens.

The Pro model features a telephoto lens that provides a 3x optical zoom capability, boasting a focal length of 77mm and an aperture of f/2.8. The iPhone 15 Pro Max features a 5x Telephoto lens, offering a focal length of 120mm. This lens is equipped with Apple's advanced 3D sensor shift optical image stabilization, which effectively stabilizes images. Additionally, Apple has incorporated its innovative tetraprism design into the lens construction. The enhanced zoom capabilities of the Pro Max result in a 5x optical zoom, surpassing the Pro's 3x optical zoom. Additionally, the Pro Max offers a digital zoom of up to 25x, outperforming the Pro's maximum digital zoom of 15x. The iPhone 15 Pro models offer enhanced video capabilities, allowing for the capture of 4K ProRes video at 60fps. Notably, this can be conveniently recorded onto an external drive connected to the iPhone 15 Pro's USB-C port. This feature streamlines the process of capturing sizable video files, alleviating concerns regarding limited iPhone storage capacity. For professionals, there are additional options available for LOG encoding, which is the established system used for configuring video color during the editing process.

The entire iPhone 15 Pro lineups uniformly benefits from the introduction of Smart HDR 5 and notable enhancements to Apple's portrait mode. In addition, the available video features remain consistent with those offered in the previous year. These include the provision of 4K video capturing capabilities at a maximum frame rate of 60 frames per second. Furthermore, users can enjoy the cinematic mode, which supports up to 4K high dynamic range (HDR) video at a frame rate of 30 frames per second. The device also offers an Action mode, along with HDR video functionality featuring Dolby Vision, capable of delivering up to 4K resolution at a smooth frame rate of 60 frames per second. Similar to the standard version of the iPhone, the device in question also boasts a 12MP TrueDepth camera positioned on the front, catering to the needs of FaceTime and other related functionalities.

The inclusion of the A17 Pro chip significantly enhances the computational photography capabilities of the iPhone 15 Pro, while the integration of USB 3 technology further contributes to its overall performance. With the enhanced transfer speeds that are 20 times faster, users now can swiftly shoot using applications such as Capture One. This enables the instantaneous transfer of high-resolution 48MP ProRAW images from an iPhone to a Mac, mirroring the seamless workflow employed by professionals.

How to Open the Camera

Here are the steps:

1. To access the Camera app, navigate to the home screen and proceed to select the Camera app.

2. To initiate access to the Camera application from the Lock screen, perform a leftward swipe gesture. Note that when accessing the Camera application from the Lock screen, it is possible to conveniently view and modify both photos and videos by selecting the thumbnail located at the lower-left corner of the screen. To facilitate the sharing of photos and videos, it is imperative to first unlock your iPhone device.

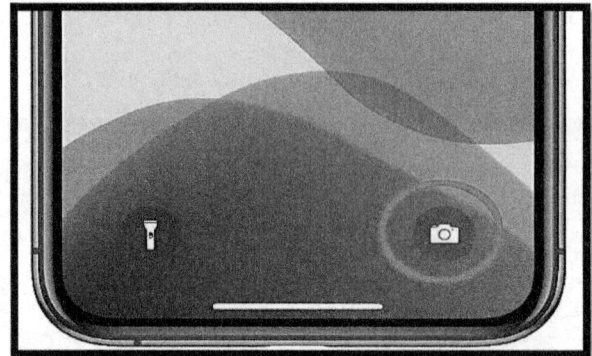

3. Use Siri and provide a command such as **"Open Camera"** to initiate the desired action.
4. On the iPhone 15 Pro and iPhone 15 Pro Max, you can assign the Action button to open the Camera application.

How to master the camera app

How to master the camera app on iPhone 15 Pro — Physical buttons

To optimize your usage of the camera app on the iPhone 15 Pro, it is essential to familiarize yourself with the physical buttons and their respective functions. By mastering these controls, you can enhance your photography experience and capture stunning images effortlessly. First and foremost, the power button, located on the side of the device, serves a dual purpose. A single press activates the screen, while a long press powers the device on or off. This button is crucial for initiating the camera app and accessing its features. Adjacent to the power button, you will find the volume buttons.

It is worth noting that the volume up and volume down buttons on an iPhone possess the capability to function as a means to capture photos, similar to a physical shutter button found on traditional cameras.

To promptly capture a photo, simply use either the upward or downward volume buttons instead of relying on the on-screen shutter button. Certain users may find this approach more convenient and conducive to minimizing phone movement during the process of capturing an image.

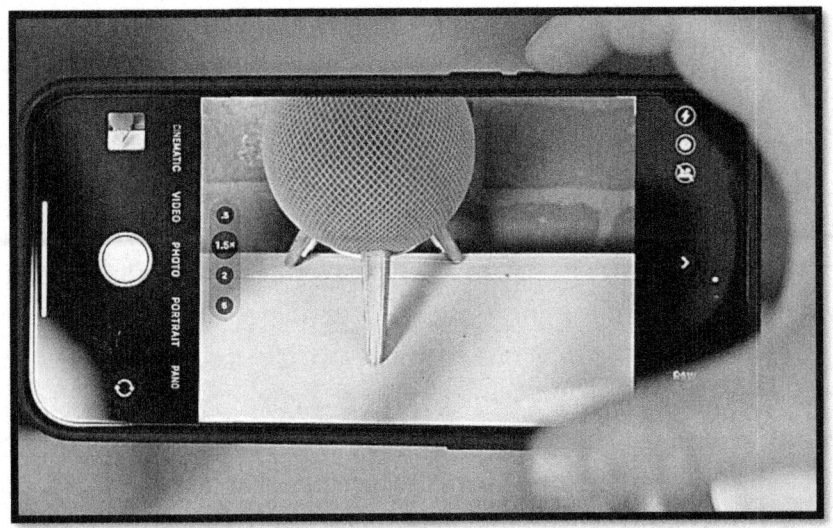

When you press and hold either button, the video recording function will begin. The on-screen shutter button transforms, assuming the form of a red circle. Concurrently, a red timer materializes at the top of the screen, serving as an indicator that a video is being recorded.

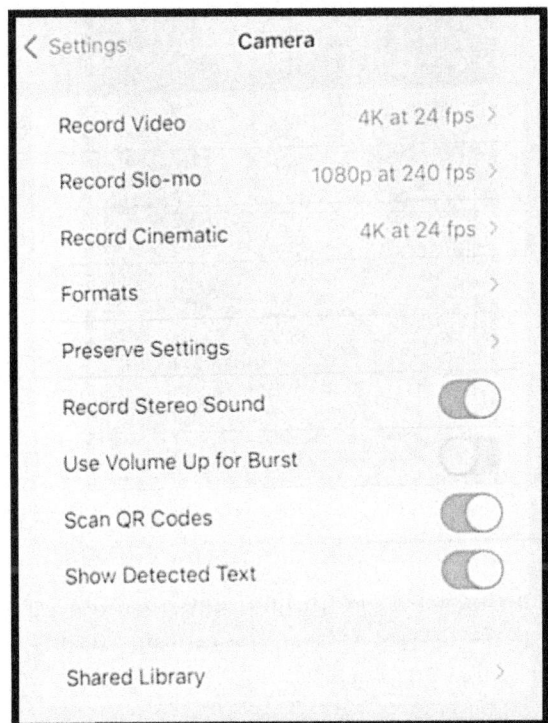

To enable the functionality of capturing burst photos, navigate to the **Settings menu** and locate the Camera section. Within this section, you will find an option to activate the use of the volume-up button for this purpose. The procedure further entails maintaining pressure on the volume down button to start video playback, while the volume up button will trigger the capture of a sequence of quick-fire photos until the button is released. Both professional-grade smartphones are equipped with the innovative programmable Action Button. Within the settings, there are various functions available for this button, such as activating the flashlight or initiating a voice memo. Given our current discussion on cameras, it is worth noting that one of the preconfigured options available for the Action Button entails launching the default Camera app. The device offers a range of modes to choose from, including photo, selfie, video, portrait, and portrait selfie. To further enhance the level of customization, users may opt to access a third-party camera application. Select the "**Shortcut**" option and proceed to "**open app**."

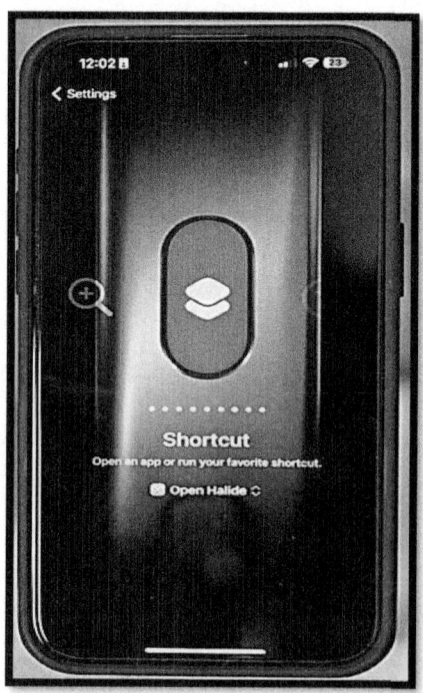

You are also free to select any third-party application of your preference. However, we highly recommend Halide due to its commendable support for cutting-edge features, including a zero-lag shutter and forthcoming compatibility with HDR technology.

How to master the camera app on iPhone 15 - On-screen controls

Within the camera application, a multitude of controls are prominently showcased, although with certain controls that may not be immediately discernible. One of them is concealed within the shutter button itself. It is widely acknowledged that capturing a photo can be achieved by simply tapping the shutter button. However, it is no surprise that there may be individuals who are not yet acquainted with the functionality known as QuickTake. The QuickTake feature enables users to seamlessly initiate burst photography or video recording without the need to switch between shooting modes.

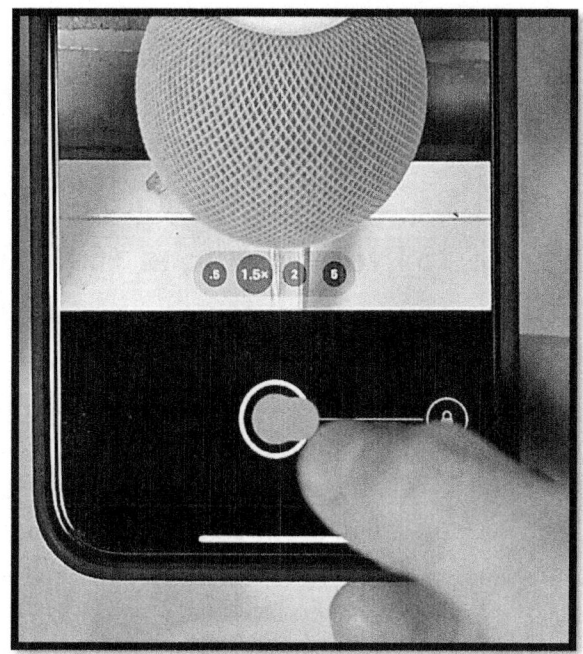

By initiating a prolonged press on the shutter button, the video recording functionality will be activated. Upon releasing the shutter button, the video capture will cease. During the process of recording a QuickTake video, it is possible to conveniently transition into video mode by sliding the shutter button towards the right. This action will effectively engage the lock feature, eliminating the need for continuous manual button pressing. Apple incorporates a captivating animation feature wherein the red square symbolizing video recording seamlessly transforms into a red circle upon dragging. The circular icon, located conveniently, can be tapped to capture a photograph while simultaneously recording a video.

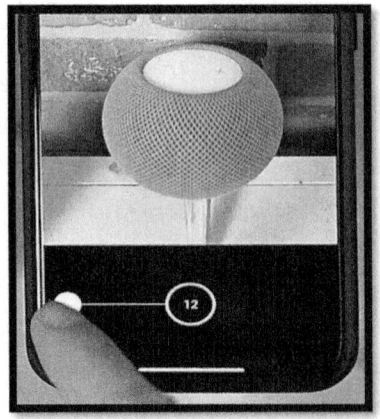

In a similar vein, initiating the capture of burst photos can be achieved by firmly pressing and expeditiously swiping the shutter button toward the left direction. When you release the shutter button, the continuous capture of images in quick succession/burst mode will stop.

Zoom levels on iPhone 15 Pro and iPhone 15 Pro Max

Both the iPhone 15 Pro and iPhone 15 Pro Max are equipped with identical sets of two main and ultra-wide cameras. The main camera offers a 1X zoom capability, while the ultra-wide camera provides a 0.5X zoom capability. The iPhone 15 Pro Max and iPhone 15 Pro exhibit a discrepancy in their optical zoom capabilities. Specifically, the iPhone 15 Pro Max boasts a 5X optical zoom on its tele lens, whereas the iPhone 15 Pro maintains a 3X optical zoom. The process of controlling them exhibits a high degree of similarity. To transition between zoom levels, simply tap any of the four on-screen buttons available, which correspond to the following options: 0.5X, 1X, 2X, and 3X/5X.

The main camera offers an additional feature wherein by tapping the 1X button, users can conveniently adjust the main zoom to either 1.2X or 1.5X. The focal lengths in question are 24mm, 28mm, and 35mm. To access the camera settings once more, you have the option to designate one of these choices as the default setting for the main camera. When you tap and hold gestures on any of the available zoom levels, users can access a granular adjustment wheel by swiping left or right. Using this feature provides users with enhanced control over the level of zoom, as opposed to relying on the pinch gesture on the screen. This method provides a convenient means of adjusting your shot using only one hand. The wheel will retract automatically upon releasing the screen, or it can be dismissed by swiping it away.

How to master the camera app on iPhone 15 - Additional controls and settings

During the process of capturing photos or videos, it is possible to navigate between various camera modes by using a left or right swipe gesture. In terms of available photography modes, users have the option to seamlessly transition between photo, portrait, and panorama. Similarly, for video recording, the device offers cinematic and slo-mo modes. The user can set focus for a photo by tapping any location on the screen, and maintaining pressure will secure the exposure. To dynamically adjust the exposure level, simply tap on your subject and smoothly slide your finger up and down. Once the fundamental concepts have been thoroughly covered, we can progress to the more intricate controls. Located at the top of the camera application interface are a variety of control options.

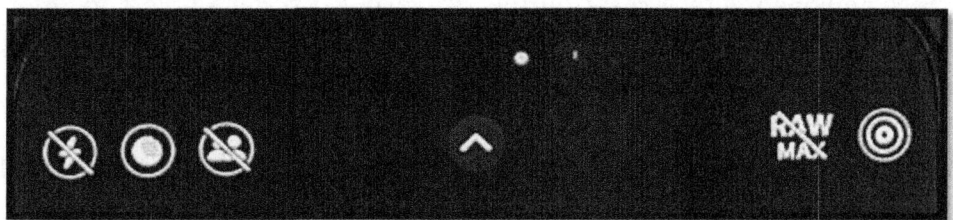

The icons positioned at the top of the application are the frequently used ones, including the flash, night mode, and shared library icons on the left side, while the Live Photos toggle is situated on the right side. When the caret is tapped in the center, it will initiate the opening of a settings tray located at the bottom of the application, positioned just above the shutter button. While certain tools may appear to be duplicated at first glance, they can provide enhanced control and functionality. The flash icon is once again present. At the uppermost section, there are solely two options available, namely "**on**" and "**off**". However, within this particular tray, you are presented with a broader range of options, including "**on**", "**off**", or "**auto**" for your selection. The night mode toggle is available, offering users the chance to adjust the duration for the shutter, in addition to the options provided at the top. The length of the adjustment will be automatically determined by the ambient lighting conditions in the room and the stability with which the phone is held.

When in motion, the camera's shutter will have a maximum duration of three seconds. However, if the phone is securely mounted on a tripod, the shutter can remain open for up to 30 seconds. The **Live Photos feature** offers three options for selection: on, auto, or off. We highly appreciate Live Photos because it can capture frames both before and after the shot, as well as their capability to animate photos post-capture. The next item in the queue is **Photographic Styles**, which is visually represented by a series of stacked squares. There are five distinct styles available for selection, namely standard, rich, vibrant, warm, and cool. The tone and warmth of each of these can be customized through adjustment. Each style is equipped with a reset button that allows users to revert to the default settings. The available settings include aspect ratio options such as 4:3, 1:1, and 16:9, exposure compensation, timer functionality, filters, and a shared library feature.

How to master the camera app on iPhone 15 - Extra shooting modes

In addition to the standard modes, there are supplementary modes available for both photography and videography that users can choose to activate. Night mode was previously mentioned and it is worth noting that it is activated automatically. However, there are a few additional modes that warrant discussion. The **macro mode feature** leverages the capabilities of the ultra-wide lens to capture photographs close to the subjects. Similar to the night mode feature, automatic activation occurs when the camera detects the proximity of the subject to the device.

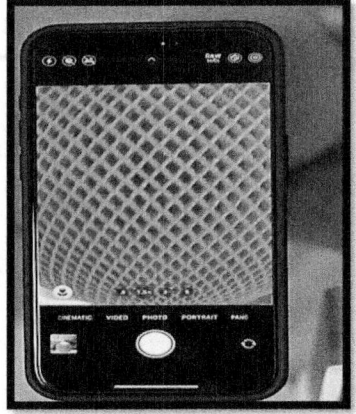

The macro mode can be identified by the presence of a small flower icon located in the lower-left corner of the interface. Within the settings of the Camera application, there exists a feature that grants the user the ability to exercise discretion in employing the macro mode. By simply tapping the flower icon, one can effectively deactivate this functionality. Now, let us delve into the topic of portrait mode. It is not always necessary to transition to portrait mode on the latest iPhones to capture a portrait image. The Camera application is designed to capture depth data for portrait shots when it detects the presence of individuals, canines, or felines within the frame. The indication of this occurrence can be identified through the appearance of a stylized letter "**f**" in the lower corner, providing the user with the ability to modify the degree of blurring.

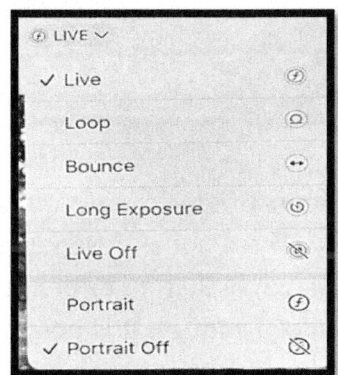

When capturing a standard Live Photo, it is possible to simultaneously capture depth data. Consequently, when viewing the photo, users are presented with the option to choose between the two available types. This situation can be described as a convergence of advantages, as it allows for the capture of dynamic moments through Live Photos, enabling pets or children to be depicted in motion. Additionally, the option to switch to portrait mode offers a visually appealing and stylized aesthetic. The Camera app still retains the Portrait mode feature, which proves to be quite advantageous when capturing images of cocktails, objects, or other animals. The action mode feature is specifically designed for capturing video footage, offering exceptional stabilization capabilities to effectively counteract excessive camera shake. To activate this feature, simply tap on the running icon while in video mode.

Video on iPhone 15 Pro and iPhone 15 Pro Max

Users can select between two distinct modes for video recording: slo-mo, which enables capturing footage at a maximum rate of 240 frames per second and Cinematic mode. Cinematic mode can be understood as a video recording format that resembles portrait mode, to a certain extent. The tracking mechanism of this device ensures that the subject remains in sharp focus, while simultaneously applying a blur effect to the background.

The user can shift the focus between different points on the screen, and this adjustment can also be made retrospectively. The iPhone 15 series has been enhanced to support video capture at frame rates of 24, 35, or 30 frames per second. For individuals seeking a higher level of expertise or enhanced control, it is possible to capture video footage in ProRes format, offering a range of color options such as HDR, SDR, or log. When the USB-C connection is established, it is possible to record video directly onto an external Solid State Drive (SSD).

How to master the camera app on iPhone 15 pro - Other settings

In addition, take into account the following additional settings that warrant attention during the configuration process of the Camera application. To optimize the quality of your photographs, it is recommended to enable the RAW format. The use of RAW format enables the preservation of a greater level of detail within the highlights and shadows of the captured images, thereby allowing users to enhance these aspects during the post-processing stage. The RAW photo settings are conveniently grouped under the "**Pro Default**" settings by Apple, providing users with the option to select from three distinct options. These include large 48MP JPEG shots referred to as JPEG Max, ProRAW photos at 12MP, or ProRAW Max, which boast a resolution of 48MP.

The latest enhancement allows for the capture of regular photos using the primary lens in an upgraded 24MP mode, as opposed to the previous standard of a compressed 12MP. Videos can be either equipped with High Dynamic Range (HDR) or lack this feature. Although HDR and Dolby Vision offer visually stunning results, their implementation can introduce complexities when editing in software such as Final Cut Pro. With the introduction of iOS 17, users now have access to an additional feature within the camera app - a level tool. This tool conveniently displays a subtle line on the screen, enabling users to maintain a perfectly level horizon while capturing photos or videos.

How to take a picture or record a video

Take a photo

- To snap the photo, open **Camera**, then hit the **Shutter button** or push either volume button.

Record videos with your iPhone camera

On your iPhone 15 Series, use the Camera app to capture videos and QuickTake videos.

Record a Video

1. From your home screen, launch the Camera app, then choose **Video mode**.
2. To begin recording, tap the **Record button** or touch either volume button. You can also do the following while recording:
   - To snap a still photo, press the white Shutter button.
   - To zoom in and out, pinch the screen.
   - To zoom in more precisely, press and hold 1x, then move the slider (on compatible models).
3. To stop recording, tap the **Record button** or hit either volume button.

When the Camera is in operation, a green dot displays at the top of the screen for your safety.

Record HD or 4K video

Depending on the type of your iPhone, you can capture video in high-quality formats such as HD, 4K, HD (PAL), and 4K (PAL).

Here are the steps:

1. Navigate to **Settings > Camera**, then choose **Record Video.**
2. Choose a video format and frame rate from the list that your iPhone supports.

Keep in mind that faster frame rates and better resolutions result in bigger video files. Also, PAL is a television visual format that is widely used in Europe, Africa, Asia, and South America.

How to Shoot Video on an iPhone: Record Professional Videos

Apple has gone a long way since the iPhone 3GS first offered video recording. Today's iPhones can shoot excellent 4K film, assist you in framing your shot, and record clear audio. You can also use the iPhone 15 Pro cameras to create high-quality commercial movies.

The tips:

1. **Set up your shot using a tripod**

The latest iPhones have optical image stabilization, which makes filming great handheld videos a breeze. However, no matter how solid your hands are, using a tripod and phone mount is superior. Consider purchasing a gimbal for your phone if you need to move around while filming. Your video will be silky smooth.

Here are some ways to assist you in steadying your shot if you're shooting handheld:

- Keep the phone near your body.
- Rest your elbows on a nearby strong item.
- Absorb bounces and shakes with your body.

2. **Choose a spot with plenty of natural light**

Shoot in a well-lit area if you want to get a great iPhone video. If you select a place with low lighting, your film will most certainly be muddy and, well, terrible. So, if at all possible, select your site with this in mind. If you're filming during the day and need extra light, attempt to match the light with white lights.

3. **Use the rear camera lenses to shoot**

Even when recording oneself, using the back camera to shoot will always appear better than using the selfie camera.

4. **Instead of pinching to zoom, move your phone closer**

Do you need to zoom in? If you have an iPhone 15 Series, use the old-fashioned method of bringing your phone closer to the subject rather than using the phone's zoom feature. This is because the iPhone's lens does not optically zoom. As a result, pinching to zoom just digitally enlarges the image. This implies you'll soon be immersed in the realm of unattractive pixelation. Moving the camera closer to what you're capturing will result in a much crisper picture. If your phone has several lenses, the ultra-wide and telephoto lenses will be useful as well. However, keep in mind that the normal 1x lens will perform best in low-light settings.

5. **Make use of your iPhone's built-in grid**

If you're unsure how to construct a good image, use your iPhone's built-in grid and frame it according to the rule of thirds.

- To enable Grid, go to **Settings > Camera** and toggle "**Grid**" on.
- Arrange your subjects such that they fall nicely on an intersecting line.
- When snapping people, make sure their eyes cross with the top line.

Note: Turn off HDR mode for video while you're in this part of your iPhone camera settings for a better-looking photo. HDR (or High Dynamic Range) is a technique used by smartphones to capture both bright and dark regions of an image. While it sounds excellent in principle, HDR footage, in our perspective, does not seem as natural. This is particularly true when snapping people. This may be an unpopular viewpoint, but if you want to be safe, keep it turned off. Another reason to avoid recording HDR is that you may have compatibility difficulties when using certain editing applications, blending HDR with SDR video, hosting on platforms, and even viewing the movie on particular devices. If you want consistency, it's just simpler to film in SDR for the time being.

6. **Use Apple Watch as a preview window**

If you have an Apple Watch, you can try this out: Make use of your Watch as a little preview window to assist you in framing your image. It's quite useful if you're shooting alone. If you don't have an Apple Watch? No worries. You can also use your phone as a preview monitor by AirPlaying it to your MacBook.

7. **Prevent automatic illumination changes by locking in exposure**

The iPhone 15 Series will focus and expose your photo automatically. This is an excellent tool for quick shots, but when capturing a video of a moving subject, it may make things very difficult. The iPhone constantly adjusts and refocuses, which might result in shaky video and lighting changes midway through the shoot. That is why we strongly advise you to use the exposure/focus lock option. It will aid in maintaining consistent focus and exposure while shooting. To focus, tap the screen, and then move the sun slider up or down to expose the photo. When you've discovered the ideal look, press and hold the focus and exposure boxes to save your iPhone camera settings. There's also a handy exposure slider if you merely want to lock in the exposure but not the focus. Slide left and right by tapping the **carrot > exposure symbol**.

8. **Use the iPhone's several shooting modes**

It's now time to be creative. The iPhone has several useful shooting options that can help your video stand out. By separating your subject with a small blur, Cinematic mode simulates the appearance of high-end movie cameras. Slow-motion mode can be used to make even the most mundane occurrences seem grandiose. Time-lapse mode, on the other hand, can show how something comes together over time, such as setting up a video shoot.

Speaking of time-lapse films, here are some helpful hints for creating a smooth one:

- Mount your iPhone on a tripod.
- Lock the focus and exposure for natural and smooth lighting changes.
- Before you start recording, put your phone on airplane mode.

9. **Do not send your videos to your computer via text or email**

Texting or sending your movies to your PC will almost always result in low-quality footage. Since movies are compressed when delivered by text or email, this is the case. For example, your 50MB video may be reduced to 3MB. That much compression will result in grainy and fuzzy video. It's a major issue since you need the highest quality footage available for the editing step. The good news is that there are methods for preserving video quality while transferring film to your computer. You can transfer the video by connecting your phone to your computer and using Image Capture. You can also AirDrop your video to your PC.

Take panoramic photos with your iPhone camera

In Pano mode, use the Camera app to capture a panoramic shot of your surroundings.

Here are the steps:

1. Launch the **Camera app** on your iPhone.
2. Select **Pano mode**.
3. Press the **Shutter button**.
4. Move the camera carefully in the direction of the arrow, staying on the centerline.
5. Finally, press the Shutter button one more time.
6. To pan in the other way, tap the arrow. Rotate your iPhone to landscape mode to pan vertically. A vertical pan may also be reversed in direction.

How to Take Photos from a Video

Have you taken a video on your iPhone 15 Series and noticed certain frames that you like and wish to save as photos to your camera roll? Don't worry. Nowadays, filming crucial events in our lives, as well as photographing them, has become virtually a habit. But what if you have a movie and want to extract photos from it on your iPhone? If you want to snap images from a video on your iPhone, free software called Frame Grabber from the software Store can assist.

Follow the instructions below to take images from your iPhone 15 movie using the Frame Grabber app:

1. First, download and install the **Frame Grabber software** from the App Store on your iPhone 15 Series.
2. Launch **Frame Grabber** and go to the video from which you want to grab one or more photos.
3. Play the video and pause it at the point/frame you want to snap.
4. Now, in the bottom right, press the share button.
5. Select the Save Image option from the menu that appears.
6. The photo's resolution will be the same as the video's resolution. Examine the EXIF data to determine the resolution.
7. Now you can shoot still shots from a video on your iPhone 15.

Capture a Still Image from a Video on an iPhone

Another easy way to get a still shot from a video on an iPhone is to go into the Camera roll and obtain the still from there:

1. To begin, go to your iPhone's Camera Roll 15.
2. Select a video and click the **Edit button.**
3. Move through the video frames and stop when you locate one.
4. Take a snapshot of the still picture by pressing the **Power + Off button** on your iPhone 15 Series.

How to change the camera modes

When you launch Camera, the default mode is Photo. Take still photos and Live photos in Photo mode.

Swipe left or right on the camera interface to choose one of the camera modes listed below:

- **Video**: Proceed to record a video.
- **Time-lapse**: Make a time-lapse movie of movements over time.
- **Slo-mo**: Create a video that has a slow-motion effect.
- **Pano**: Take a panoramic photo of a landscape or other subject.
- **Portrait**: Use a depth-of-field effect in your photographs.
- **Cinematic**: Add depth-of-field to your videos.
- **Square**: Shoot images in a square ratio.

Tap ⌃ on iPhone 15 Series, then select 4:3 to choose between Square, 4:3, and 16:9 aspect ratios.

How to Capture Log Footage on an iPhone 15 Pro Versions

The iPhone 15 Pro and bigger iPhone 15 Pro Max family of phones have a variety of camera features, including the option to shoot in Log mode. The iPhone 15 Pro is the first model in Apple's flagship phone series to support the format, which is ideal if you want to take film and then color-grade it later. This is a function that should be disabled unless you want to grade the film since ordinary Log video appears drab and flat. It is not enabled by default, but you can enable it by following the instructions below.

Requirements:

- An iPhone 15 Pro or 15 Pro Max

Here are the steps:

1. First, unlock your iPhone 15 Pro or iPhone 15 Pro Max. This will not function with the ordinary iPhone 15, nor will it work with earlier Pro or Pro Max devices.
2. Locate and open the **Settings app**.
3. Scroll down to Camera and touch it once you're in Settings.

4. Next, scroll down to the Formats option and select it.

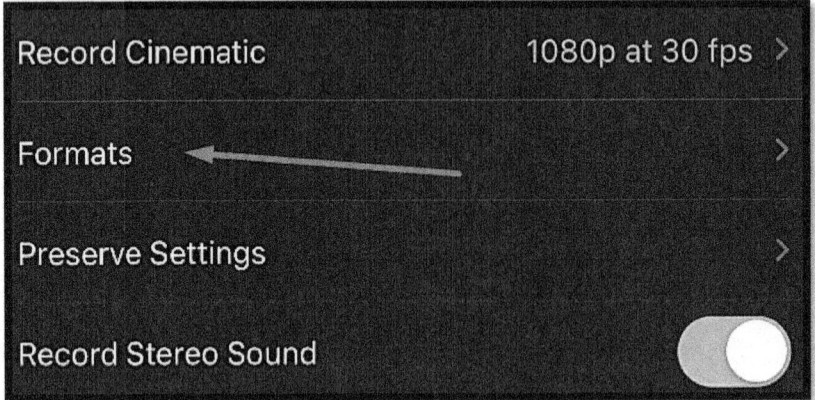

5. Before you activate Log, make sure ProRes is turned on. This should be enabled by default, but if it isn't, change the Apple ProRes option to green.

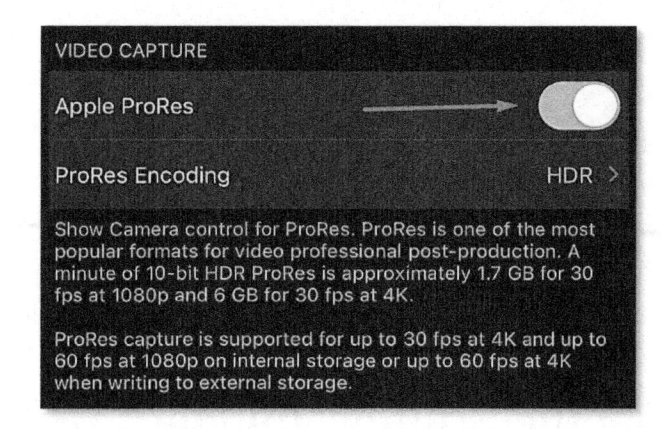

6. There is another option called ProRes Encoding under the Apple ProRes option. You'll be directed to another menu if you tap this.
7. There are three options in the ProRes Encoding menu: HDR, SDR, and Log. HDR is the default, but clicking Log will make Log the default. 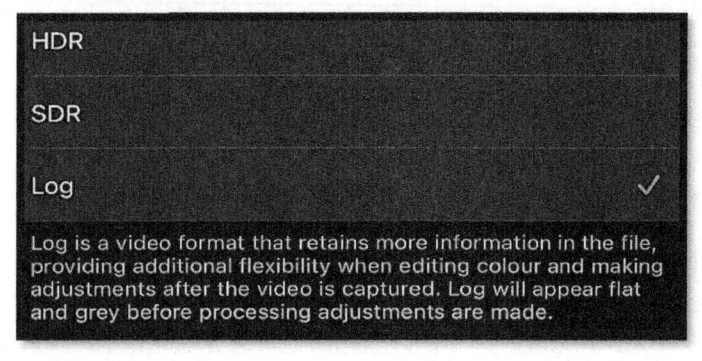
8. Now just close **Settings** and return to the Camera app. On the top menu bar, there is a ProRes Log option; press it to switch modes. Tap it once more to turn it off.

How to zoom in and zoom out

Here are the steps:

1. Open the Camera app on all models and squeeze the screen to zoom in or out.
2. To swiftly zoom in or out on iPhone models with Dual and Triple camera systems, such as the iPhone 15 Series, choose between 0.5x, 1x, 2x, 2.5x, 3x, and 5x. Touch and hold the zoom controls, and then move the slider right or left for a more exact zoom.

How to Adjust the Shutter Volume

Simple Methods to Turn Off Camera Sound

Apple has worked hard over the years to ensure that its camera quality is better than those of competitors as well as previous versions. However, while using the camera app, customers are experiencing shutter sound issues. Since the shutter sound disturbs them, users often look for how to turn off the camera sound.

The different methods include the following:

Turn on Silent Mode

Apart from the operating system, the Ringer or Silent button distinguishes the iPhone from other devices. This function is available on all iPhone models and is quite handy if you wish to silence your iPhone. To turn off the camera sound on the iPhone 15 Series, follow the instructions below.

- To begin, users should glance at the upper left corner of their iPhones.
- You can locate the Mute, Ringer, or Silent button here.
- Slide the ringer button from top to bottom. This is a simple process.
- Next, you'll see a little quantity of red above the button. This means your iPhone is presently in quiet mode.
- Now that you've set your iPhone to silent mode, you can take images without making a sound. This is the easiest way to learn how to disable the shutter sound on iPhone 15.

Enable Live Photos

Turning on the live photos feature while snapping photographs in the camera app is another easy way to learn how to turn off the iPhone 15 camera sounds. When you use this function, your phone's shutter sound will be disabled. The Live Photos control in the current version of iOS is represented by a sequence of circles at the top right of the screen.

To disable camera sound on the iPhone 15, use the Live Photos function as described below.

- To begin, launch the camera app on your iPhone.
- To enable the Live Photo function, click the sequence of circles symbols.
- Subsequently, click the arrow in the upper center to choose between Auto, On, and Off.

- Once enabled, you can now take photos on your iPhone model without hearing the shutter sound.

Reduce the volume of your iPhone under the Control Center

If you do not wish to take images in Live Photo mode, there is another way to turn off the camera sound. The Control Center allows you to adjust the volume. However, before you use the Camera app, be sure you turn down the sound. If you're running iOS 17, scroll down from the upper right-hand corner to open the Control Center. You can reduce the volume after the Control Center is opened. You will now understand how to disable the camera sound on the iPhone 15 Series.

While the music is playing, take photos or screenshots

Another loop or workaround for eliminating camera shutter noise is to use a different sound. Do not be perplexed. You may listen to music while taking a shot and your camera's sound will not be muted. If you don't want the music to play, just put in a headset or connect it to wireless headphones. As a result, any noise (whether from music or the camera shutter) will be muffled since it will be heard via the headphones.

While recording videos, take photos or screenshots

This is still another way that might assist you in resolving the to turn off camera sound iPhone 15 problem. All you have to do is launch the **Camera app** and choose **Video mode**. Begin recording the video by hitting the **Record button** in the bottom center. The photo-shutter button will appear once the recording begins. All you have to do is press the shutter button. This will take images while filming and will not interfere with the video.

How to Change the HDR Camera Settings

Changing the HDR camera settings

HDR (high dynamic range) in Camera assists you in capturing stunning images in high-contrast settings. IPhone takes numerous shots at various exposures in fast succession and blends them to add more highlight and shadow detail to your images.

When it's most effective, the iPhone captures images in HDR (for both the back and front cameras) by default. The iPhone 12 and 13 models, as well as the iPhone 14 and 15 models, record HDR video to capture true-to-life color and contrast.

Disable automatic HDR

When HDR is most effective, the iPhone uses it by default. Instead, you can tweak HDR manually on select iPhone models. On the iPhone XS, iPhone XR, iPhone 11 models, iPhone SE (2nd generation), and iPhone 15 models, go to **Settings > Camera**, then turn off Smart HDR, and then press HDR to switch it off or on from the camera screen.

Turn off and on HDR video

For true-to-life color and contrast, iPhone 12 models, iPhone 13 models, iPhone 14 models, and iPhone 15 models capture video with Dolby Vision HDR. To disable HDR video recording, go to **Settings > Camera > Record Video**, and then disable HDR Video.

How to customize the main camera lens

The default for the 1x Main camera lens on the iPhone 15 Pro and iPhone 15 Pro Max is 24 mm. You can add secondary lenses of 28 mm and 35 mm and select which lens is the default Main lens.

Here are the steps:

1. Navigate to **Settings > Camera > Formats > Photo Mode**, and then choose 24 MP.
2. Navigate to **Settings > Camera**, then choose **Main Camera**.
3. Turn on the lenses you want to use as extra Main lenses under extra Lenses.
4. Tap the choice you wish to use for the default Main lens underneath the Default Lens.
5. To quit Settings, swipe up from the bottom of the screen.

After you've selected your main camera lens, click the **Camera button**. Depending on your decision, the default lens for the Main camera will be 1x (24 mm), 1.2x (28 mm), or 1.5x (35 mm). Switch between the other lenses by tapping the Main camera lens.

Top 5 iPhone Camera Settings for Better Video Quality

Capturing high-quality video material with your phone is as simple as point-and-shoot; however, optimizing your video content for multiple platforms — from social media to personal computer storage — requires a deeper grasp of certain settings. You can create visually striking videos with a professional touch by fine-tuning critical elements such as resolution, frame rate, High Dynamic Range (HDR) video, grid settings, out-of-frame views, macro control, and stabilization, as well as applying basic shooting and exposure methodologies. This short and simple procedure will help you to quickly learn these approaches.

1. **Change to 4K Resolution**

This is a must-do and the most important recommendation for ensuring a significant quality improvement. The newest iPhone models are capable of recording in 4K quality. The detail in this advanced video option is four times that of 1080p HD video. Switching your iPhone 14's camera to 4K resolution will greatly improve the quality, sharpness, and detail of your recordings. This makeover will give your film a professional appearance and feel, letting it stand out on networks such as Instagram or TikTok. Whether you're recording a family reunion, an outdoor trip, or a business assignment, the 4K setting will capture every scene in breathtaking clarity. Open the Camera app, change the camera mode to Video, and then look at the bottom right corner of your screen. You'll notice an HD label if you're filming in 1080p. To convert to 4K video, just tap HD.

2. **Shoot at a frame rate of 24 frames per second**

Frame rates are more important than you would believe. For example, to improve the cinematic and visually engaging quality of your movie, configure your iPhone to record at 24 frames per second (fps). This is not a random number; 24 frames per second has long been the industry norm, contributing greatly to what people commonly connect with the 'look' and 'feel' of professional cinema. The camera's settings are often set to the conventional 30 frames per second; however, many specialists would disagree. The idea is that 24 frames per second accurately simulate how the human eye sees motion in real life, resulting in a more realistic viewing experience. This frame rate adds a beautiful appearance and a real feeling of authenticity to your films, improving their overall impact.

Adjust the default resolution and frame rate from 720p at 30fps, 1080p at 30fps or 60fps, and 4K at 24fps, 30fps, or 60fps by going to **Settings > Camera > Record Video**.

3. **Turn off "HDR Video"**

HDR video can improve visual quality by displaying brighter highlights, more brilliant colors, and a wider variety of tonal nuances. This improvement is especially obvious in certain settings, such as recording pictures with dramatic contrasts between bright and dark areas. While it may seem that continually enabling the HDR Video function is the best option, it's crucial to realize that its use may result in unforeseen consequences in some situations. Colors might seem too saturated or unnatural in HDR, particularly in settings that do not demand high-contrast improvements. The image seems grainy at times and overcompensates for movement. Disabling the HDR Video function on your iPhone while recording videos is sometimes suggested achieving color uniformity and a natural appearance across your clip.

4. **Turn on the Grid**

When recording videos, one feature you may not have explored yet but should get acquainted with is the "**Grid**" function. When engaged, this helpful feature shows a grid overlay on your screen when filming movies. This grid is based on a photography and videography technique known as the rule of thirds. If you're unfamiliar with the rule of thirds, it's a basic but powerful composition approach that divides your frame into nine equal portions by a set of horizontal and vertical lines. But how can this assist you? By putting your primary subject or crucial pieces along these gridlines or at the junction spots, you may produce a more balanced and interesting image. This approach is often used to direct the viewer's gaze and provide depth and complexity to an image.

5. **Disable the "View Outside Frame" option**

Distractions are the last thing you need when you're attempting to catch the ideal photo. That's when the "**View outside Frame**" option on your iPhone comes in handy. Though it might be useful in certain instances, it can also be a problem in others. When this option is activated, you may see what's immediately beyond the frame of the movie on your screen. While it is useful for planning your next camera move, it may also draw your attention away from the main subject of your video. Turn off the "**View outside Frame**" option when you truly want to focus on your subject and eliminate any unwanted distractions. In this manner, your screen will only show the precise frame captured by the camera, allowing you to remain focused on your subject. It's similar to putting blinders on a horse—it enables you to focus entirely on what's ahead.

6. **Enable Stabilization**

As much as we'd all want to have the calm hands of a seasoned cinematographer, the fact is that our films may sometimes appear more like a roller coaster ride than we'd like. When engaged, the stabilization function works its magic to reduce camera shaking and offer smoother, more stable video footage. Consider it like having an unseen helper that assists you in keeping your camera steady, smoothing out any unintended bumps or wobbles that may otherwise make your video seem wobbly. Activating the stabilization function may make a difference whether you're walking through the park, filming your dog's joyful activities, or recording a gorgeous bike trip. It guarantees that your movies seem stable and smooth even while you're moving.

7. **Basic Exposure and Shooting Techniques**

Great tutorials don't stop at the settings menu; go beyond the fundamentals and provide further assistance with popular accessories or suggestions.

Lighting

Let's discuss your lighting game. It is critical to constantly be aware of your surroundings and the lighting conditions. Seek out well-lit places, and don't be afraid to use artificial lighting when necessary. Be wary of very strong light sources that might cause overexposure or create harsh shadows—they're more hassle than they're worth.

Composition

Let's get creative with composition next. Keep the rule of thirds in the back of your mind while you frame your photos. Consider your screen to be split into a three-by-three grid, and try positioning your subject off-center—trust me, it will improve the visual attractiveness of your composition. Make your subject the star of the scene, not simply a part of it. A single touch on your screen may bring them to the forefront. Do you want to keep them there? Simply push and hold until the AE/AF Lock indication appears. It's like handing your subject a special invitation to the in-focus party.

Better Exposure

Maintain the brightness of your video by manually changing the exposure. Simply touch the screen and move the exposure control up or down. It's especially useful as the illumination starts to change.

White Balance

Let's discuss using a white balance to establish the atmosphere. It's all about harmonizing the colors in your movie to the lighting circumstances. While the Auto option is ideal for most scenarios, manual changes are useful when you need greater control over the color temperature. It's similar to painting but with pixels.

Frequently Asked Questions

1. What are the new camera features in the iPhone 15 Series?
2. How do you open the camera app?
3. How do you master the camera app?
4. How do you take a picture or record a video?
5. How do you take panoramic photos with your iPhone camera?
6. How do you capture photos from a video?
7. How do you change the camera modes?

CHAPTER TWO
VIDEO RECORDING

Overview

Chapter two discusses everything that has to do with video recording from recording a QuickTake video to recording a time-lapse video and the like. Read on to learn about the different video recording options in your iPhone 15 Series.

How to record a QuickTake video

Using an iPhone to take a picture or record a video is simple and quick. You can even use the camera app without having to unlock your phone. However, if you want to shoot a video, you may need to make an extra effort to discover the video mode on the camera menu before you can record. That was before the introduction of QuickTake. You can now capture videos quicker than ever before. QuickTake on the iPhone 15, iPhone 15 Plus, iPhone 15 Pro, and iPhone 15 Pro Max allows you to swiftly capture movies. On previous iPhone models, you had to scroll through the camera menu to locate the Video option, then push the red button to begin recording. With QuickTake, there is now a new quicker method to take video.

If you're wondering how to use QuickTake on the iPhone 15 Series, follow the instructions below:

1. For a quicker method, launch your iPhone's Camera app from the home screen or touch the camera symbol at the bottom of your lock screen.
2. When you open the Camera app, the photo mode will be shown by default. To begin recording, press and hold the white shutter button for a few seconds, then release it. Yes, the picture mode's shutter button may now be used to shoot video.
3. Slide the button to the right to lock the recording and capture a longer movie without pushing the shutter. The shutter button has been relocated to the right side. By touching it, you can use it to shoot images while recording a video. Tap the **recording button** to end the video recording.

How to Use QuickTake for Taking Burst

Before QuickTake was introduced to the iPhone 11 series, all you had to do to capture burst photographs was hit the shutter button in Photo mode. However, since that button is meant to record a video, you cannot use it to take a burst shot. Moving the shutter button to the right allows you to lock the video recording while moving it to the left activates burst mode. If you want to capture a burst shot, move the shutter button to the left.

Shoot QuickTake with the volume up button

When you were in photo mode, long-pressing the volume up or down button on the side of the iPhone would send it into continuous shooting mode. The photos were shot one after the other in fast succession as he did so. If your iPhone is among those on the list, this gesture has been replaced with QuickTake video capture. However, with iOS 17, you can use the volume buttons to switch between continuous shooting mode and QuickTake mode, needing just one setting to be changed along the way. Press and hold the volume up button to continuously shoot if you want the volume up button to be held down. As a result, if you use the switch Button to raise the volume of the series outside means that holding down the button will take a video.

How to record a time-lapse video

A time-lapse video is a compressed video of an event that takes place over time. It's a series of still photographs captured every few seconds to create the illusion of a sped-up video. Time-lapse is ideal for recording images that would take too long to observe at ordinary speed, such as a sunset, ocean tides, a plant leaf unfurling, or city traffic during rush hour. Because they are quick and frequently amusing, time-lapse films are popular, particularly on social media. Time-lapse videos are a lot of fun, particularly when they are used to record a slow natural movement, such as the sun rising or setting, or you may produce a time-lapse video of moving clouds. It doesn't stop there; it may be used to photograph any natural phenomena. The iPhone's time-lapse function will not allow you to record films longer than 30 seconds, thus even if you record a video for an hour, it will be time-lapsed to only 30 seconds.

Here are the steps:

1. Launch the **Camera app**.

2. Swipe through the shooting modes until you reach time-lapse.

3. Tap the screen area you want to capture. This will focus the iPhone camera on your subject automatically.
4. After pressing, you can change the exposure on the iPhone camera to make the video darker or brighter by swiping it up or down.

5. To start and stop the time-lapse movie, use the red Shutter button.

Time-lapse photography is very sensitive. To capture an event, keep the iPhone in situ and extremely motionless for at least 30 seconds (preferably 30 minutes or more). When you're finished recording, the video will display in your Photos app.

Experiment with Time-Lapse in Night Mode

You can now shoot time-lapse films in Night mode on the iPhone 15 Series. Simply begin filming time-lapse in low-light circumstances, and Night mode will activate immediately. You can also now monitor the moon and stars throughout the night, catch the motions of a busy metropolitan night, or watch your bonfire burn down to embers.

Change the camera's video recording settings on iPhone

The camera captures video at 30 frames per second (fps) by default. Other frame rates and video resolution choices are available depending on your iPhone model. Larger video files arise from faster frame rates and greater resolutions. You can also modify the video resolution and frame rate immediately on the camera interface by using quick toggles. To modify the video resolution and frame rate, use the quick toggles. Use the quick toggles at the top of the screen in Video mode to modify the video resolution and frame rates available on your iPhone. Depending on your model, use the quick toggles in the top-right corner to select between HD or 4K recording and 24, 25, 30, or 60 fps in Video mode. Quick toggles in Cinematic mode on iPhone 14 and iPhone 15 models allow you to move between HD or 4K and 24, 25, or 30 fps.

Change the Auto FPS settings

In low-light settings, the iPhone may enhance video quality by automatically lowering the frame rate to 24 fps.

Go to Settings > Camera > Record Video, and then perform one of the following:

- Select **Auto FPS**, and then set it to just 30-fps video or both 30- and 60-fps video.
- Enable **Auto Low Light FPS**.

Turn on and off the stereo recording

- To create stereo sound, the iPhone has several microphones.

- To disable stereo recording, go to **Settings > Camera** and uncheck **Record Stereo Sound**.

Turn off and on HDR video

IPhone captures HDR video on eligible models and distributes HDR recordings with devices running iOS 13.4, iPadOS 13.4, macOS 10.15.4, or later; other devices get an SDR version of the same video.

- To disable HDR recording, go to **Settings > Camera > Record Video**, and then disable HDR Video.

Turn Lock Camera on and off

The Lock Camera setting on iPhone 13 models, iPhone 14 models, and iPhone 15 models prohibits automatic switching between cameras when recording video. By default, the Lock Camera is turned off.

- To enable Lock Camera, go to **Settings > Camera > Record Video**, and then enable **Lock Camera**.

Turn on and off Enhanced Stabilization

The Enhanced stability option on iPhone 14 and iPhone 15 models zooms in significantly to give enhanced stability when filming in Video and Cinematic modes. By default, Enhanced Stabilization is enabled.

- To disable Enhanced Stabilization, go to **Settings > Camera > Record Video**, and then **disable Enhanced Stabilization**.

Turn on and off Lock White Balance

When shooting videos on your iPhone, you can lock the white balance to increase color capture accuracy dependent on lighting circumstances.

- To enable Lock White Balance, go to **Settings > Camera > Record Video** and choose **Lock White Balance**.

How to Change iPhone Time Lapse Settings

The simplicity of the iPhone's built-in time-lapse capability is its charm. If you're serious about time-lapse photography, you'll want greater control over the settings on your iPhone. Several excellent time-lapse programs allow you to customize the settings. You may, for example, modify the iPhone time lapse speed to slow down or speed up the clip. You have control over how many photographs are collected each second. You may also postpone the start of the recording. Some time-lapse software even allows you to add music or voice-over to your films. Following that, you'll learn how to manipulate your time lapse settings with the Hyperlapse and OSnap applications. You can modify the pace of your time-lapse recordings using Hyperlapse. OSnap allows you complete control over your iPhone's time-lapse settings. Once you've become acquainted with each app, you can choose which iPhone time-lapse app best meets your requirements.

Tips to make a perfect Time-lapse video on iPhone

Apple does not provide any option for creating a flawless time-lapse film on iPhone; you may just shoot the video and then stop it. However, by following these guidelines, you can create superior time-lapse films on your iPhone.

- **Adequate Time**

Make sure you have enough time to film the footage before you begin generating the time-lapse movie. For instance, if you're on a beach and want to capture a time-lapse movie of the sun sinking. Allow at least 10-15 minutes to get the ideal time-lapse movie.

- **Sufficient iPhone Battery**

Also, make sure your iPhone has adequate battery life to capture a time-lapse film. We can't provide an exact amount since it varies by model and the state of your iPhone's battery.

- **Make use of a tripod stand**

As previously said, shooting a time-lapse movie might take a long time, thus we strongly advise you to use a tripod stand to capture the video. It will not only eliminate flickering but will also make it easier to film time-lapse videos.

- **To capture time-lapse videos, use the Perfect App from the App Store**

There are several applications available to assist you in capturing Time-lapse films on your iPhone, but some of them are just outstanding. You can use either Lapse it or Timelapse. Unlike the native functionality of camera apps, these apps provide a plethora of options. Settings in programs allow you to choose the duration of the recording, the final length of the video, and even the Time speed. The nicest aspect about both programs is that they are both completely free.

How to record a slow-motion video

Slow-motion clips add drama to your films, and you can make them with little more than your iPhone. You can shoot in Slo-mo using your iPhone's Camera app, but you can also slow down a previously recorded video.

How slow motion works on iPhone

When you capture a slow-motion movie on your iPhone, you are playing back the footage at a reduced frame rate, giving the impression that the video is going slower than it is in real life. The Slo-mo function may be used to capture fascinating natural landscapes, sports footage, and strong action shots. Slo-mo has been a regular function on iPhone camera models since the iPhone 5S. Simply open the Camera app on your iPhone and navigate through the menu above the shutter button to reach Slo-mo. You're ready to go when you tap Slo-mo!

What is the speed of an iPhone slow-motion video?

An iPhone's standard viewing speed is 60 frames per second (FPS). If you want to record more footage in a slow-motion movie, you should film it at a greater frame rate. Slow motion emerges when high-frame-rate film is slowed down. All iPhone models that support Slo-mo will capture movies at 120 frames per second (half the standard pace). Newer versions (iPhone 8 and later) with the A11 Bionic CPU can capture Slo-mo films at 240 FPS, which play back at one-quarter regular speed.

Shooting slow motion using an iPhone camera

Now that we've cleared the air, let's attempt some shooting methods and advice for making great slow-motion videos. You won't be able to stop experimenting once you start.

How to Change iPhone Slo-mo Settings

Before we begin shooting films, let's have a look at your iPhone's settings. The FPS and quality of your video will be determined by the iPhone model you're using. You can set your Slo-mo settings to the maximum quality for the greatest effects, but be warned: these incredible films will take up a lot of space on your phone.

Here's how to change your iPhone's slow-motion settings:

1. Go to Settings on your iPhone.
2. Scroll down and choose **Camera**.
3. Select **Record Slo-mo**.
4. Select the maximum frame rate for the greatest effects, but keep in mind that this will take up more space on your phone.

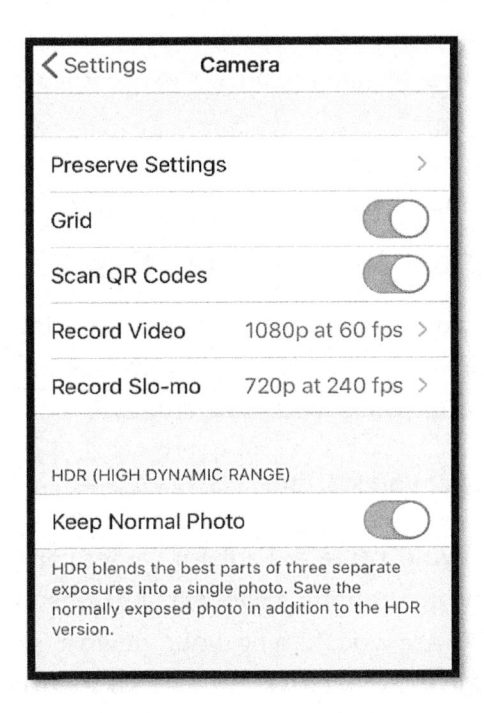

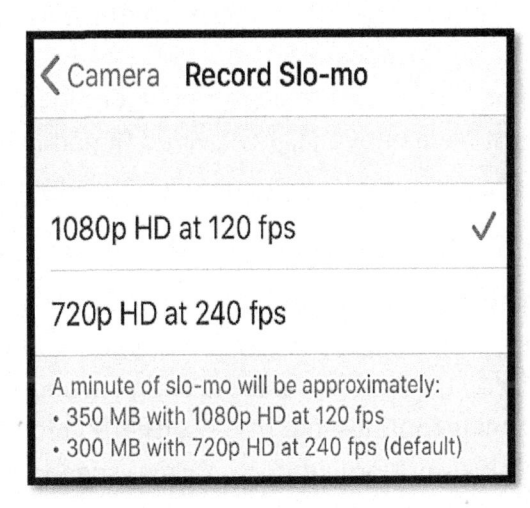

How to shoot a slow-motion video with your iPhone

Here comes the exciting part. Follow the steps below to shoot slow-motion videos with your iPhone 15 Series camera:

1. Open the **Camera app** on your iPhone.
2. Tap **Slo-mo** to activate the slow-motion option after scrolling through the shooting modes above the shutter button. You can only use Slo-mo with your iPhone's rear camera unless you have an iPhone 11 or newer.
3. When you're ready to start filming, press the red **Record button** or one of the side volume buttons.
4. Tap again to end the recording.
5. Save your slow-motion movie to your photo library.

How to Make Your Slow Motion Video Pop

You may have learned the fundamentals and tried a few slow-motion pictures of your children playing in the sprinkler or your dog racing through the woods, but if you want your Slo-mo films to stand out, you'll need to be creative.

Here are some pointers to get you started:

- **Change the angle of your camera:** Look for camera angles that will showcase the action for more impact. Shooting a snowball into the air? Capture it as it whizzes toward the camera. Are you filming your newest skateboard trick? Set your camera at a low angle to get a bird's-eye view of the road and wheels.
- **Consider the video sound**: When you slow down the playback speed, take in mind that the sound will also slow down.
- **Shoot in bright light**: Since you are capturing your video at a greater frame rate than usual, you must have enough light. A video filmed in low light will look much darker.

How to convert normal video to slo-mo

After you've captured some good slow-motion footage, you can apply modifications to make your films truly stand out – modify the speed of your video, crop it, trim it, or use filters to change the style. You thought you were making a wonderful slow-motion film of your friend's incredible dancing routines, but the results aren't flattering. Fortunately, you can quickly convert your slow-motion video to normal-speed video with a few screen touches.

Here's how to go about it:

1. Open your **Photos app**, choose the **Slo-mo video** you want to edit, and then hit **Edit**.
2. There are two sliders at the bottom of the screen. The first displays the frames from your video. The second displays when your movie transitions from normal to slow motion.
3. Drag the vertical white line across the second slider until the lines are all the same width apart. This will return the Slo-mo sections to normal speed.

4. If you just want to adjust a segment of your movie to standard speed, move the slider in either way.

5. When you're happy with the results, click **Done**.

How to speed up a slow-motion video

If you want to speed up your video even quicker than usual, you'll need to utilize iMovie, which is available for free on the App Store.

Here's how to use iMovie to speed up your slow-motion video:

1. Launch **iMovie** from your iPhone.
2. On the welcome page, tap **Continue**.
3. Tap + to begin a new project, then **Movie**.
4. Select the slow-motion video to edit and hit **Create Movie** at the bottom of the screen.
5. Tap the video to bring up the editing tools.
6. To speed up your movie, use the speedometer indicator.
7. A slider with a turtle on one end and a rabbit on the other will emerge. Sliding this toward the rabbit will double the pace of your movie.

8. To see your findings, press the **play button.**
9. At the top of the screen, tap **Done**.

How to slow down your video

You can use iMovie to slow down or speed up your Slo-mo movie. Simply follow the same steps as before, except this time drag the slider toward the turtle rather than the rabbit to slow down your movie.

How to trim, crop, and straighten your slow-motion video

The Photo app on your iPhone contains some rudimentary editing tools that you may use to tidy up your slow-motion videos. You can simply cut, straighten, and crop iPhone movies using these tools.

Here's how to go about it.

1. To begin, open the slow-motion video you want to modify and choose **Edit**.
2. Trim the movie by dragging the arrows at each end of the timeline slider toward the center. To make your video shorter, you may cut it at the beginning or finish.

3. Tap the crop symbol to straighten your video. To use the straighten function, touch the circle with the horizontal line across it. Move the slider to the right to straighten your video.

45

4. Crop your video to the appropriate size by hitting the crop button and dragging the boundaries of your movie.
5. Click Done.

How to adjust exposure, contrast, and color for a Slo-mo video

The iPhone Photos app can also alter the look of your slow-motion movie by modifying the exposure, contrast, and color using individual sliders or ready-to-use filters.

Here's how to use these enjoyable editing features in Photos:

1. In Photos, choose the video you want to modify and then select **Edit**.
2. Select the edit icon, which is a circle surrounded by little dots.
3. Above the slider are several icons that will alter the appearance of your movie.
4. The exposure indicator is a circle with a plus/minus sign within it. Tap here and then move the slider to adjust the exposure.
5. To access the contrast slider, press the **contrast symbol**, which looks like a black-and-white circle cut in half. To adjust, move the slider back and forth.
6. To increase the saturation, select the saturation icon (a colorful circle) and drag the slider to the desired color saturation.

7. To apply a filter to your movie, press the filter icon (three linked circles) and navigate through the available selections.
8. Select Done when you are through.

How to use action mode

On the newest iPhones, Action Mode is a powerful video stabilization feature. It is intended to compete with specialist action cameras such as the GoPro and hardware options such as a gimbal. Apple is notoriously secretive regarding its technology; however, we do know that Action Mode uses the full camera sensor. It then takes into account sophisticated roll correction to provide buttery smooth footage even while moving.

For aspiring home cinematographers, Action Mode now supports Dolby Vision and HDR. You may also note that when you launch Action Mode, the ultrawide lens is selected by default. This is done for a variety of purposes, the most essential of which is to provide more light. Since Apple's thorough post-production and editing sometimes result in somewhat darker films, it's preferable to begin in a bright setting. Another advantage is that the ultrawide camera allows the iPhone to crop more effectively. If your shot's edges are wobbly, the iPhone may reduce them for a better outcome. Regrettably, iPhone owners who want to make movies will have to invest in the newest technology. So far, Action Mode is only accessible on the iPhone 14 and 15 series, with no plans for backward compatibility. It takes far longer to explain Action Mode than it does to get the functionality up and running.

Follow these steps to get started with your action star dreams:

1. Launch the **Camera app**.
2. Select the **Video option**.

3. To enable Action Mode, tap the tiny running figure in the upper left corner.

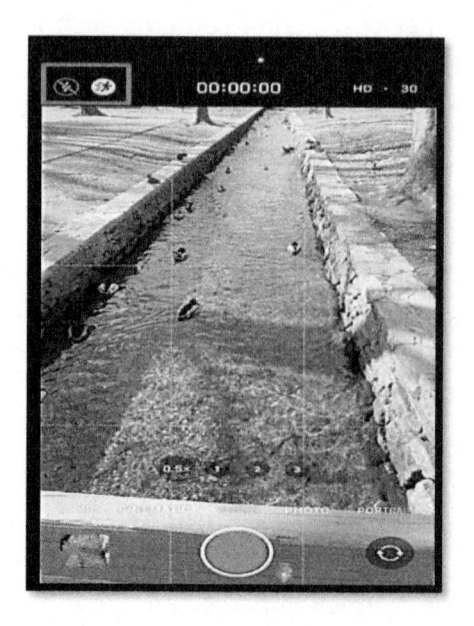

If everything is in order, you should see a little yellow symbol in the corner and an Action Mode indication on your screen.

How to customize Action Mode

When left to its normal settings, Action Mode is ideal for bright daytime footage. However, there are situations when you prefer smaller, more manageable files or just cannot get enough light. If you find yourself in any of these situations, you must be aware of Apple's camera settings. It's simple to customize your camera to your heart's desire.

Follow the steps below:

1. Launch the **Settings app**.
2. Navigate to the **Camera** section.
3. Select the **Record Video option**.

You can then choose your video quality and frame rate, as well as turn Action Mode Lower Light on and off. It's a self-explanatory function that lessens overall stabilization so you can still use action mode when there isn't as much light available.

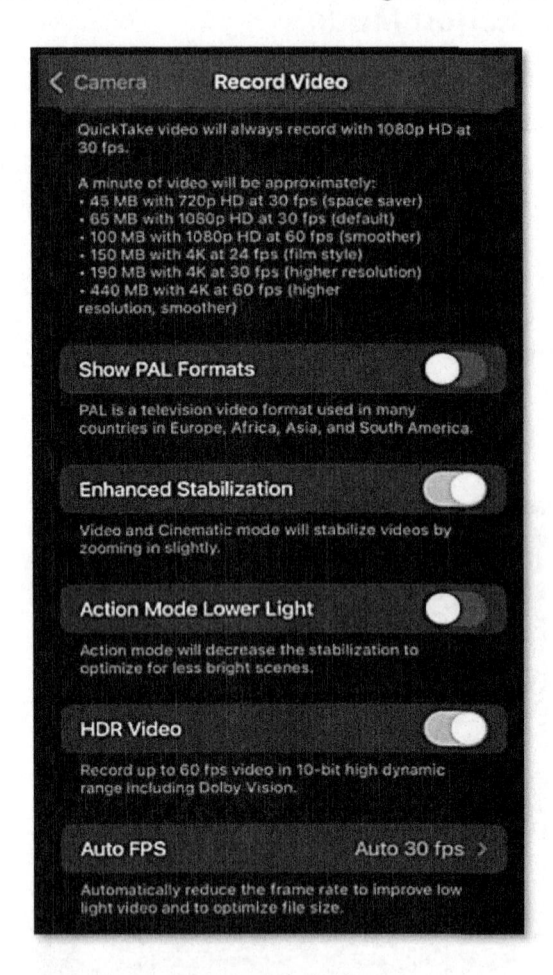

Frequently Asked Questions

1. How do you record a QuickTake video?
2. How do you use QuickTake mode for taking bursts?
3. How do you use time-lapse video mode?
4. How do you change the camera's video recording settings
5. How do you record a slow-motion video?
6. How do you convert normal video to slo-mo?
7. How do you speed up a slow-motion video?
8. How do you use and customize action mode?

CHAPTER THREE
RECORDING IN PRORAW AND PRORES

Overview

This chapter specifically focuses on using your iPhone 15 Series to record in both ProRAW and ProRes formats and how to get the best out of the two formats.

How to record in ProRAW and ProRes on the iPhone 15 Pro and 15 Pro Max

ProRAW and ProRes are professional file formats developed by Apple that let you keep as much information as possible in your photos. While it will not enhance your first preview, you can use this additional information when editing your images to give you more options when modifying parameters like white balance, exposure, contrast, highlights, and more. ProRAW captures are 10-bit files that employ the linear DNG format to preserve the extra information in photographs taken with your camera. ProRes is a 10-bit lossy compression video format composed of codecs that is widely used by video editors and cinematographers. It provides increased data and editing information for use in post-production while keeping your file sizes to a bare minimum. Although these professional formats are excellent for capturing photographs and films from your iPhone 15 Pro, they are not suitable for daily use. Here are a few pros and cons to assist you in deciding whether to use these formats on your iPhone 15 Pro and Pro Max.

The Benefits of Using ProRAW and ProRes

- 10-bit files with great sensor data retention.
- More flexibility in post-production to edit and improve your captures.
- Increased Dynamic Range allows for more precise color editing.

Disadvantages of using ProRAW and ProRes

- Large file sizes might lead to a lack of storage capacity.
- You'll need to change your files each time to get the desired appearance and depth.

- ProRes 4K recording at 30 frames per second is only available on iPhone 15 Pro and Pro Max models with 256GB, 512GB, or 1TB storage.

- If you desire 48MP photos, you can only take ProRAW images at 1x.
- ProRAW photos in night mode, macro, and flash are always 12MP.

How much space are ProRAW and ProRes capture going to take up?

According to Apple's estimations, ProRAW and ProRes captures on your iPhone 15 Pro and Pro Max will be around the following size.

- **ProRAW images** range in size from 25MB to 28MB (48MP captures).
- **ProRes Videos**: One minute of HDR ProRes video in HD (1080p) takes up 1.7GB. 1 minute of 4K HDR ProRes video is 6GB.

How to Capture in ProRAW

You must first activate ProRAW on your iPhone before taking photos with the Camera app. Here's how to do it on the iPhone 14 Pro and Pro Max.

Turn on Apple ProRAW

- Tap **Camera** in the Settings app.
- Now, at the top, choose **Formats**.

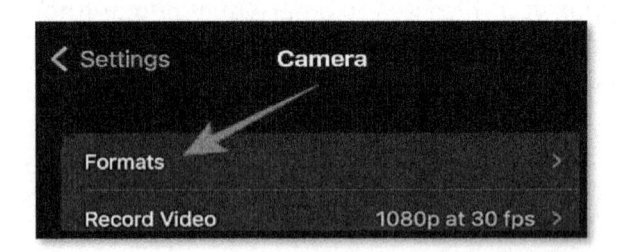

- Turn on Apple ProRAW by tapping and holding the toggle.

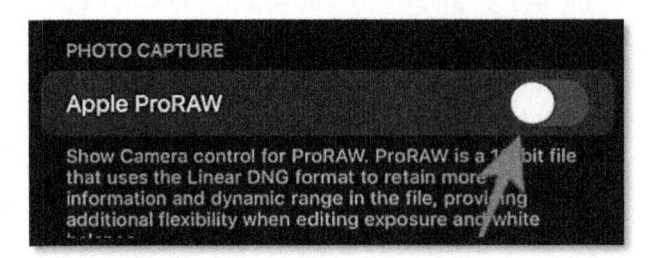

- Choose **ProRAW Resolution**.

- Tap and choose **48MP**.

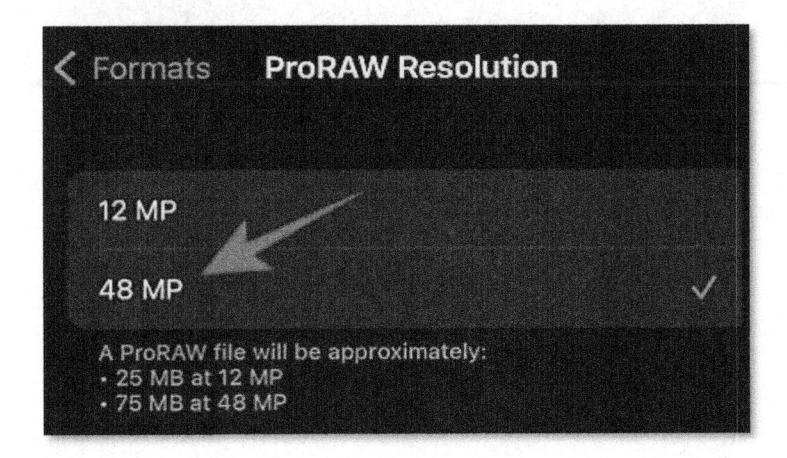

- Close the **Settings app** and go to the following phase to capture photographs in ProRAW, which will now record 48 MP images without binning them.

Take RAW pictures

- Open the Camera app and pick **Photo** at the bottom. Now, in the upper right corner of your screen, hit the RAW (RAW) symbol.

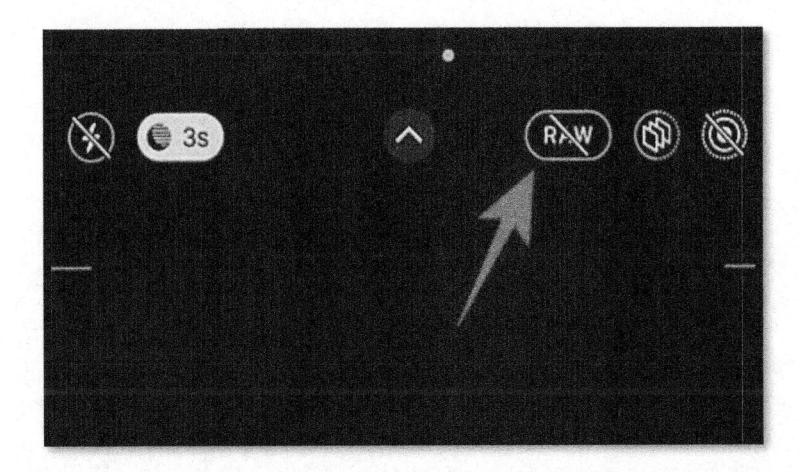

- After you've activated RAW (RAW), frame and take your picture as required.

- In the Photos app, you can now verify the image's details. If recorded in 1x typical illumination, your picture should now be 48MP in terms of resolution and size. If you use the flash, Night Mode, Macro, or any other lens combination other than 1x, the RAW picture will be binned down to 12MP.

How to record in ProRes on iPhone 15 Series

To record in ProRes, you must first activate ProRes on your iPhone, as you would with ProRAW. Use the instructions below to guide you through the procedure.

Enable ProRes

- Tap **Camera** in the Settings app.
- At the top, choose **Formats**.
- At the bottom of your screen, tap and activate the Apple **ProRes toggle**.

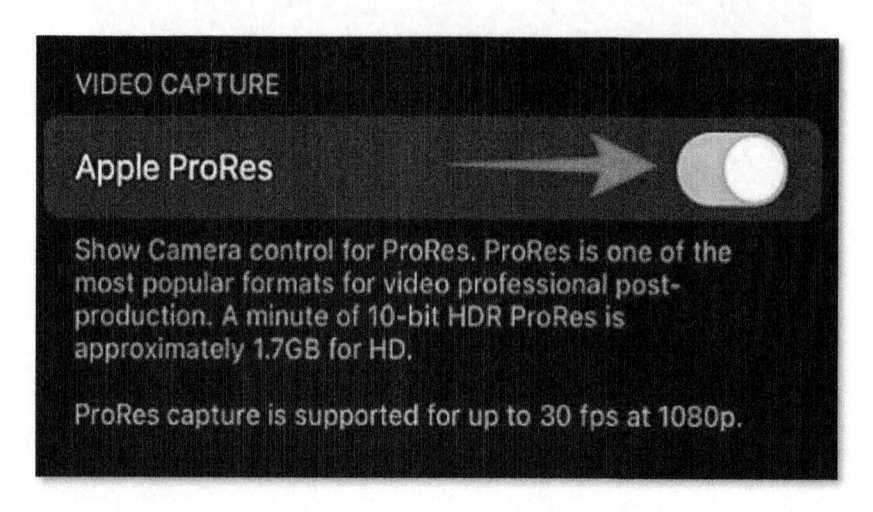

- Return to the previous page and choose **Record Video**.
- From the options at the top of your screen, tap and choose your chosen resolution and FPS.

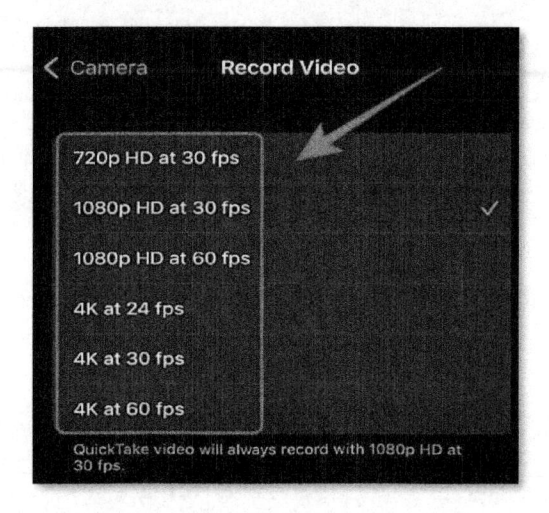

- Note that if you have a 128GB model, you can only shoot ProRes films in 1080p HD at 30 frames per second or less.
- You can now uninstall the Settings app. Your iPhone now supports ProRes. Use the following section to record the ProRes video on your iPhone.

Record in ProRes

Once you've activated ProRes on your iPhone 15 Pro or Pro Max, here's how to record in it.

- Open the **Camera app** and scroll down to **Video**.

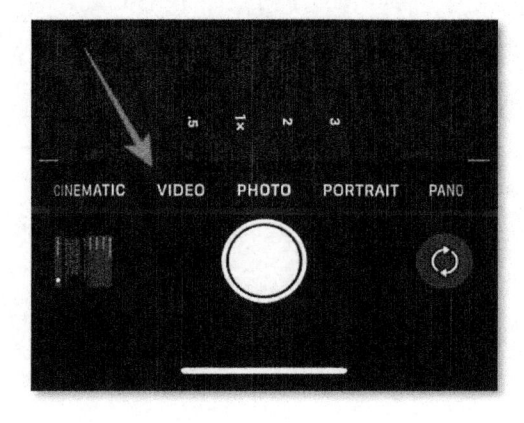

- To enable ProRes capture, hit the toggle for **ProRes** (ProRes) at the top.

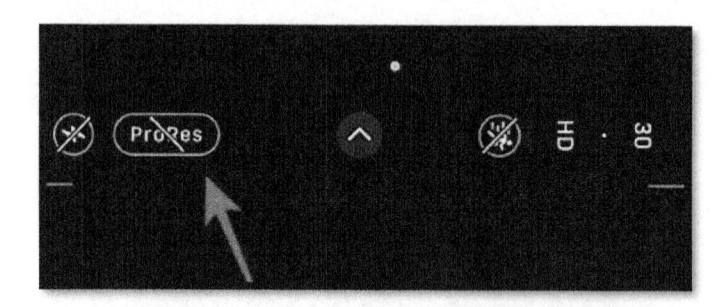

- The maximum duration for which you can record a video will now be shown at the top, depending on the available storage space on your iPhone.

- To record your video, tap the **shutter symbol**. When you're finished, tap the symbol again to end the recording.

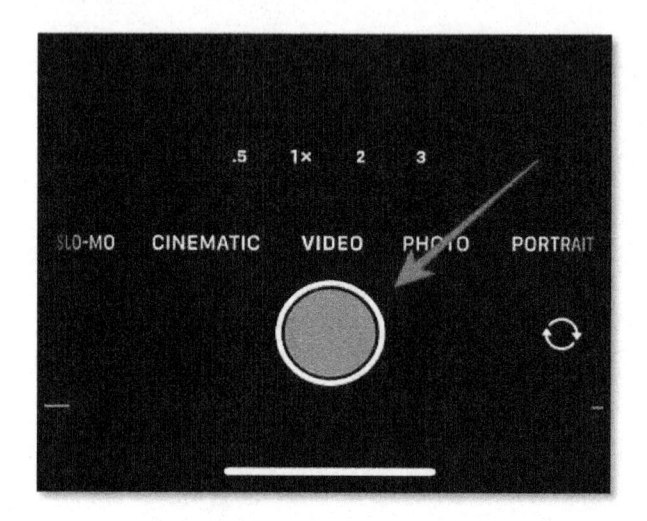

Top iPhone 15 Pro & Max Accessories for Filmmaking

If one's passion lies in the world of filmmaking, it is imperative to carefully contemplate the acquisition of various products that will undoubtedly facilitate and enhance their cinematic endeavors. Simplify your filmmaking process and elevate your videography skills with the following suggestions. Using an iPhone filmmaking kit will elevate the quality of your visuals to a professional standard. If you are seeking products that offer exceptional sound quality, this list also includes recommendations in that regard.

- **SmallRig Video Cage for iPhone**

Enhance your filmmaking endeavors with the SmallRig Video Cage iPhone filming kit, offering a fresh and captivating experience. This comprehensive kit is designed to streamline your workflow and elevate your creative output, ensuring a seamless integration into your professional filmmaking endeavors. For vloggers and creators, the Pro Cage kit offers exceptional functionality. It features strategically placed mounting holes that facilitate seamless live-streaming processes. Additionally, it provides an optimal angle for capturing stunning photos or videos. The kit includes various mounting options that enable users to securely attach their phone to either a tripod or a stand, complete with robust grips and lighting features. By utilizing this iPhone filming accessory, users can optimize the available features such as the ability to attach a microphone, LED lights, tripod, and other compatible accessories. The mount rig cage, which is conveniently accessible, can be effortlessly inserted. My iPhone serves the same purpose as a protective phone case. Users will encounter no obstacles in their iPhone usage and will be able to achieve unrestricted access to their devices. This iPhone accessory is an essential tool that filmmakers should not overlook.

- **Moment Blue Flare Anamorphic Lens for iPhone**

This lens product offers an exceptional opportunity to elevate the quality of your photos or videos. It represents a highly advantageous proposition that is tailored to meet your specific needs. The use of a Moment phone case is a requirement for the optimal functioning of this product, albeit one of its drawbacks. This product facilitates the seamless mounting of your lens using a Moment Case mount. The product is compatible with dual phone camera lenses, allowing users to optimize their photography experience. Additionally, the Moment Camera Application offers the functionality to de-squeeze videos, enabling users to fully use the product's capabilities. This accessory offers an enhanced photography experience for iPhone users, making it an exceptional choice for filmmakers seeking to elevate their craft. The product can capture visually captivating images and can be adjusted to achieve the desired aspect ratio. Given the numerous advantages associated with this product, it is evident that it holds a position of high desirability. The Moment Blue Flare lens is a valuable tool for professional photographers and videographers. If you fall into this category, we highly recommend acquiring this exceptional device without delay.

Rode VideoMic Me Compact TRRS Cardioid Microphone for iPhone

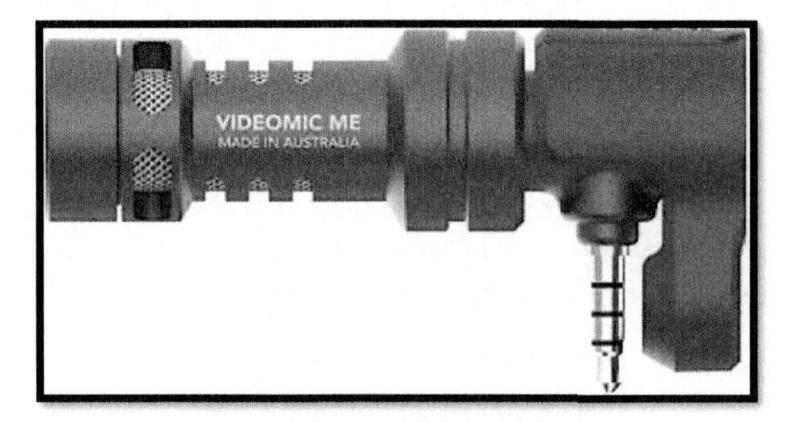

This compact TRRS microphone is specifically designed for iOS devices, making it an efficient solution for individuals who frequently conduct meetings using their iPhones. The product boasts a frequency range spanning from 100 Hz to 20 kHz, rendering it highly versatile. Additionally, its lightweight design further enhances its appeal. The device features a 3.5mm headphone output and boasts conveniently accessible dimensions. The product features a high-quality outdoor shooting deluxe furry windshield that effectively mitigates adverse weather conditions, ensuring optimal performance. This particular product has been widely favored by customers, undoubtedly. This microphone is guaranteed to provide optimal audio quality when used with your iPhone. Hence, if one consistently encounters challenges in achieving optimal audio quality, we highly recommend acquiring a Rode VideoMic to enhance and sustain an uninterrupted audio experience. Hence, it is advisable to promptly proceed with the acquisition of this advantageous product.

- **Sony Folding Professional Closed Ear Headphones**

Experience unparalleled sound quality with the Sony professional studio headphones, meticulously designed to deliver an exceptional audio experience. These headphones are equipped with neodymium magnets, renowned for their ability to produce powerful and dynamic sound output. These headphones offer a combination of comfort and lightweight design, coupled with exceptional noise cancellation capabilities for effectively blocking out ambient sounds from the surrounding environment. The cord can extend up to a maximum length of 9.8 feet, providing enhanced convenience for the user. The package also includes an adapter. We highly recommend this product for individuals who frequently engage in travel, as these headphones possess the convenient feature of being effortlessly foldable and storable within a supple case. The exceptional quality of its construction ensures optimal outcomes while minimizing the potential for any harm. Ensure that you do not overlook this exceptional product that guarantees an unparalleled sound experience with its crystal-clear sound quality. This accessory is an essential addition for individuals who engage in performance art or have a passion for music, particularly those who partake in DJing.

- **Crane for Camera and iPhone**

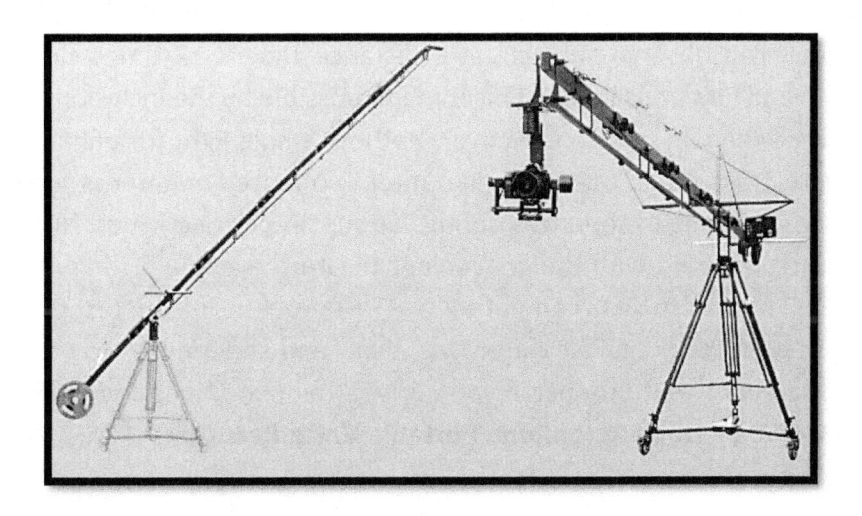

Are you in need of a durable and dependable camera crane that offers versatility in capturing different angles during film or video production? If you need a solution to fulfill your motion video filming requirements, the PROAIM 21ft Alphabet Professional Jib Boom Crane would be a suitable choice. The camera crane exhibits exceptional power and sturdiness, owing to its construction using aircraft-grade aluminum materials, thereby guaranteeing its long-lasting durability and resilience. The installation process for this crane is conveniently uncomplicated, as it is accompanied by a comprehensive step-by-step manual and requires no additional tools for assembly. Experience the ability to effortlessly capture or record exceptionally smooth and high-definition videos, thanks to the incorporation of ribbed sections and reinforced joints. These design features enhance the overall durability of the device, providing it with four times the strength to effectively minimize any unwanted shocks or shakes during operation. The enhanced durability of the fork facilitates seamless maneuverability of the crane across a wide range of angles. The innovative tilt lock feature allows for capturing stable shots and offers versatile height options of 21 feet, 18 feet, 15 feet, and 12 feet, catering to various filming needs. The fully assembled crane is packaged in a foam-padded bag, providing enhanced protection and ensuring optimal portability for convenient transportation to any desired location.

- **Monocular Telescope**

Suppose engaging in avian observation is among your preferred recreational pursuits. In such circumstances, the Gosky 12×55 High Definition Monocular Telescope proves to be highly suitable for individuals engaged in outdoor wilderness exploration and those who possess a strong passion for such activities. A portable device that is essential for engaging in activities such as bird-watching, wildlife observation, hunting, hiking, mountaineering, camping, surveillance, and traveling. The product boasts a 12×55 high power magnification, providing optimal viewing capabilities for your outdoor excursions. With this feature, you can observe subjects at a distance that is 12 times closer, all while enjoying a crisp and luminous image. This is made possible by the inclusion of a generous 55mm objective wide lens, which effectively gathers ample light for enhanced visibility. The high-powered monocular telescope guarantees enhanced brightness and exceptional clarity for optimal viewing experiences during various outdoor activities. Notably, its long eye-relief feature, coupled with the convenient twist-up eyecup, distinguishes this top-tier monocular set from its competitors. The process of argon purging offers comprehensive protection against water, fog, dust, and shocks, thereby enhancing the durability and safety of your product in various weather conditions and environments.

- **Deity V-Mic D4 Duo Microphone Portable Voice Recorder**

For individuals who have a keen interest or are actively engaged in vlogging, it is imperative not to overlook this exceptional and conveniently obtainable product. The utilization of a portable voice recorder can significantly enhance your workflow, as it allows for seamless integration of voice recording while engaging in video creation activities. The superior audio quality offered by this voice recorder will significantly reduce your workload to an unprecedented extent. The product features a dual cardioid pickup pattern and incorporates advanced low-noise circuitry. This device also provides an auxiliary input for connectivity. The shockproof and highly durable nature of this product from Deity renders it an appealing purchase option. The device in question is widely regarded as a top choice among vloggers.

- **Apple Headphone Jack Adapter**

If you possess an iPhone, it is highly recommended to acquire this particular accessory from Apple. This 3.5 mm headphone jack adapter facilitates the connection of audio devices by replacing the charging port, thereby enabling a seamless and uninterrupted music-listening experience. The audio jack of the iPhone 13 Pro Max is not only compatible with this specific device but it can also be used with any Apple device that supports the lightning charging port. To properly connect your headphones, please ensure they are securely attached to the designated location. Next, insert the headphone jack into the charging port of your iPhone. This Apple accessory is designed to enhance user convenience by providing a solution for iPhones that lack a built-in headphone jack.

- **Rode Wireless GO II Compact Wireless Mic System**

This Rode device is highly regarded and recommended for individuals who frequently conduct interviews, as it greatly simplifies the process and enhances efficiency in this professional setting. It is imperative for interviewers to thoroughly review this information. This particular wireless microphone is designed for two-person interviews and boasts exceptional sound quality. The product is equipped with two compact clip-on transmitters and recorders, offering a user-friendly setup process. Due to their reliance on electronic charging, these wireless microphones offer a guaranteed battery life of at least seven hours. The USB interface functionality of this product is highly commendable, instilling confidence that users will encounter no errors or mishaps when utilizing these wireless microphones.

- **Overhead Stand for your Apple iPhone**

The Arkon Pro Phone or Camera Stand is a specialized phone mount stand that has been specifically designed to cater to the needs of smartphone users, pico projector users, and individuals utilizing small to medium-sized cameras. This stand offers a distinctive feature of providing a stable overhead view, which proves to be highly advantageous for capturing photographs or streaming live video content related to various hobbies such as stamping, baking, pottery, and other craft-related activities. The pole of this overhead stand can be conveniently extended from a minimum height of 17 inches to a maximum height of 29 inches. This feature allows for capturing optimal overhead shots using your phone, small camera, or mini projector. The HD8RV29 Pro Stand by Arkon features an overhead arm assembly that incorporates three flexible shafts, offering users four adjustment points to achieve optimal positioning flexibility. Obtain unobstructed overhead views by utilizing the straightened-out overhead arm assembly, which extends approximately 12.5 inches away from the base of the stand. This configuration ensures that overhead views are free from any obstructions. The Pro Stand features an overhead arm assembly that offers the flexibility to bend down to a minimum distance of 2 inches from the table surface. This capability enables users to capture high-quality photographs or videos of small or intricate objects with ease.

The Arkon Pro Stand boasts a height of 43 inches, making it an ideal choice for individuals seeking to stream live video in a standing position or capture images of tall or large objects. The Arkon Pro Stand is equipped with an optional camera adapter, which is provided as part of the package. This adapter is specifically designed to accommodate small cameras and other devices that possess a ¼ inch-20 pattern connection. The camera adapter is versatile and compatible with both mini and pico projectors, enabling the projection of patterns and images onto various surfaces, including cookies and other creative projects. The Pro Stand also boasts a robust weighted base that offers a stable and secure platform for various multimedia applications such as video recording, photography, Instagram or Facebook Live sessions, as well as lives streaming or video conferencing from any location.

- **Joby GorillaPod Compact Tripod Stand**

The tripod exhibits unprecedented stability and versatility. This highly adaptable product enables users to securely grip, wrap, and maintain its standing position. Additionally, it incorporates a convenient mechanism for swiftly wrapping its legs. The tripod stand facilitates efficient and reliable securing of camera equipment, ensuring optimal durability. The product offers a 360-degree bending capability and a 90-degree tilting feature for enhanced convenience. This iPhone videography accessory is highly recommended, and the tripod stand is compatible with GoPro devices. Additionally, the GoPro can be effortlessly mounted onto this tripod, allowing for seamless integration with microphones. Doesn't that sound sufficiently exhilarating already? Indeed, it is. We highly recommend acquiring this versatile tripod as it will significantly enhance your daily workflow, elevating it to new heights.

How to remove objects in photos

The steps are as follows:

- To remove an object from a photo, use the **Photos app** on your iPhone and choose the appropriate snap.
- Tap the "**Edit**" button in the top right corner of the screen. The editing interface will open as a result.
- The item removal options accessible to you may differ depending on the model and operating system of your iPhone. A common option is the "**Markup**" or "**Retouch**" tool. Consequently, you are expected to be using the latest Apple software.
- To acquire a more realistic view, zoom in on the area that contains the item you want to eliminate. To expand, squeeze your fingers together.

Remove the Object

- Using your finger or a stylus, trace over the item you want to erase. This action should highlight the object with the selected area.
- Once you've picked an object, look for the option that allows you to remove or retouch it. On certain iPhone models, this may need the use of the "**Heal**" or "**Repair**" options.
- Check the image after the removal to ensure that the item was removed correctly. If not, repeat the removal process or use an eraser tool.
- Make any necessary changes to ensure that the edited area blends in flawlessly with the rest of the image.
- When you are satisfied with the results, tap the "**Done**" button to save the edited picture.

In contrast to the original

- Holding down the "**Edit**" button displays a comparison of the untouched and edited images.
- Drag your finger or use the slider to compare the original and revised versions.
- If you are pleased with the edited image, tap "**Save**" to commit the changes.
- If you want to save the original picture, you can also select to save it as a new copy.

How to record cinematic video

When recording video, Cinematic Mode uses Dolby Vision HDR and a technique known as **"rack focus"** to fluidly transfer the emphasis from one subject to another. To produce depth of field, it locks the focus on the subject in an image while blurring the surroundings. When you move the camera to focus on a new subject or a new subject enters the picture, Cinematic mode adjusts the focal point to this new subject and blurs away the background. For example, if you're filming someone and a second person joins the frame, your iPhone will automatically alter the background blur to concentrate on the second person. It will even return to the original subject if the person's face moves away from the camera, thereby creating a sophisticated professional filmmaking effect on the fly. Video in Cinematic Mode on iPhone 15 series devices can be captured in 1080p at 30fps. Apple updated the Cinematic mode for the iPhone 15 series, allowing it to record in 4K at 30fps and 4K at 24fps. While the Cinematic feature is remarkable, it isn't perfect; fortunately, Apple has made the effect changeable, owing to a post-shoot editing feature that allows you to change focus points after you've taken footage.

How to Shoot Videos in Cinematic Mode

The steps:

1. Open the **Camera app** on your iPhone and choose "**Cinematic**" from the camera mode menu.

2. Align the viewfinder so that your original subject and the focal point of the lens are in focus, then press the Shutter button to start recording the video.

3. Allow another person or item to join the image from a different distance away from the camera lens - your iPhone will automatically refocus when it latches onto the new subject. When you're finished recording the video, press the **Shutter button** once again.
4. After you've filmed your video, you can also manually pick the subjects you want to focus on.

How to Adjust Cinematic Mode Focus Post-Shoot

Follow the steps below:

1. Open the **Photos app** on your iPhone and choose a video that was filmed in Cinematic style.
2. In the top-right corner of the screen, tap **Edit**.

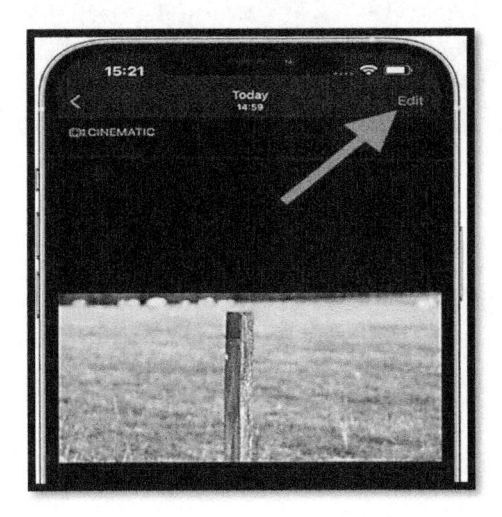

3. Drag your finger down the clip reel at the bottom of the screen to choose the section of the clip you want to change.

4. Tap a different part of the photo to change the attention point to a different subject. The indicator in the top-left corner of the screen is now highlighted, indicating that Manual Tracking is enabled.
5. The dotted yellow line below the clip reel displays the length of time the presently chosen subject is monitored in the clip. If you press the circled dot on the line, a trash symbol will emerge; tap this to erase the tracking for this subject.

6. When you're satisfied with your modifications, tap **Done**.

How to trim a video

When it comes to producing and sharing videos with your iPhone, particularly when it comes to editing, there may be a steep learning curve. You don't require expensive editing software for simple operations like trimming or shortening films and removing unnecessary segments. In reality, the majority of basic video editing activities can be completed in either the Photos app or iMovie.

Trimming a Video in the Photos App

The Photos app is not a complex video editing tool, but it does allow for some simple video adjustments when all you need is a fast tweak before posting to social media. Trimming a movie to make it shorter is something that the Photos app accomplishes extremely effortlessly. **You can cut from either end of your video clip using the Photos app by following these steps:**

1. Launch the **Photos app** and choose the video you want to edit.
2. Select **Edit**.

3. At the bottom of the screen, tap the **video camera icon**.

4. Did you see the slider under the video? To efficiently shorten your video clip, hold your finger on any of the arrows and move it inward.
5. When you have completed the process, press **Done**.
6. A pop-up menu will display. Depending on your options, choose Save Video or Save Video as New Clip.

Trimming an iPhone video for Instagram

Are you posting your video on Instagram? Move the yellow slider bar on either side of your clip inside the timeline at the bottom of the screen to keep films under Instagram's length constraints. On the main video screen, you'll be able to check how lengthy your video is.

Here's a rundown of Instagram's video length restrictions:

- **Instagram Stories**: Each Story card may be up to 60 seconds long. If you post a lengthier video to Stories, it will be automatically divided into shorter bits.
- **Instagram Posts**: Any video published as an Instagram Post can last between 3 and 90 seconds.

How to cut a video on iPhone into parts

Using the Photos app, you can trim a video into individual pieces, which is great if you want to generate numerous short films for various reasons.

This is how it works:

1. Open your iPhone's **Photos app** and choose the video you wish to edit.
2. Slide your finger over one of the arrows on each side of the video timeline to alter your clip.
3. Play your footage and make any required adjustments.
4. Select **Done**.
5. A drop-down menu will display. Tap the **Save Video as New Clip button**. To save several snippets as separate videos, return to the original video and repeat the preceding steps for each clip.

How to Use iMovie to Split and Rearrange Clips

The approach described above is excellent for repurposing your clips, but what if you want to trim and rearrange segments inside the same video? The simplest approach to divide and rearrange clips is using iMovie.

Here's how to go about it:

1. Launch **iMovie** on your iPhone and choose or add the video clip you wish to trim.

2. The timeline will show underneath your video. The playhead is the vertical white line where any current editing will take place. Move the playhead with your finger to the point where you wish to cut your video.
3. Tap the playhead, then at the bottom of the screen, and select **Split**.
4. iMovie will make a transition between the two freshly made clips.
5. Drag the clip you want to shift to the left or right on your movie timeline with your finger. Remove your finger from the clip once it is in the appropriate place.

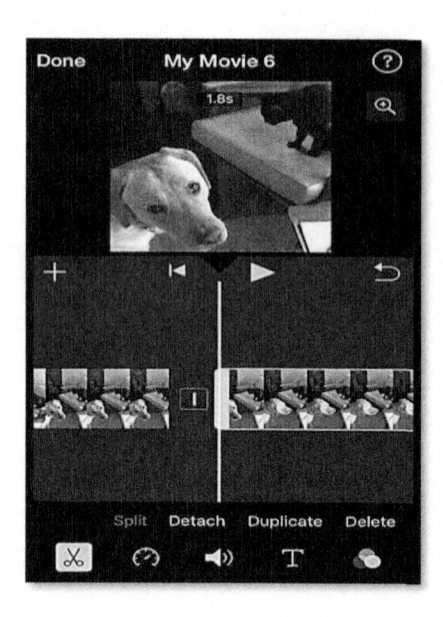

6. Select **Done** to save your film to iMovie.
7. Select the upload icon to add your movie to your picture collection.

How to cut a clip out of a video

Here's how to cut a clip out of a video:

1. Launch **iMovie** and select the **Add icon** to import your video clips.
2. After you've selected your video clips, press **Create Movie**. The chronology will show underneath your movie on the screen.
3. Navigate through your timeline until you reach the beginning of the scenario you wish to erase.
4. Tap the playhead, and then **Split**.
5. Continue to play the tape until you conclude the scene you want to erase.
6. Tap the playhead once more and then **Split**.

7. The deleted clip will now be divided on both ends. Tap the clip to highlight it in yellow.

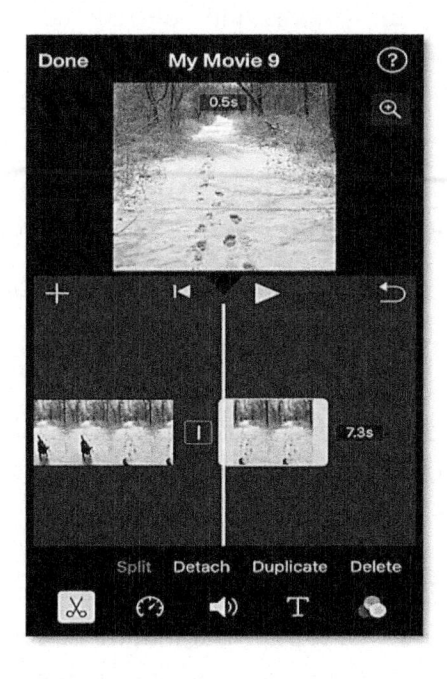

8. Select **Delete** to delete the clip from your video.
9. Tap **Done** to save your film in iMovie.
10. Tap the upload symbol and then save the movie to save your movie to your picture library.

How to record the screen

Have you ever wished to record a video of your iPhone screen to highlight a fantastic app or a handy feature? There are multiple ways of recording the screen and we will be highlighting them individually below:

Add the screen recorder to the control center

- On your iPhone, launch the "**Settings**" app.
- Scroll to the bottom and touch "**Control Center**."
- Look for "**Screen Recording**" under "**More Controls**," then press the green plus (+) icon next to it. The Screen Recording option will now be available in your Control Center.

- Once done, open **Control Center** by swiping down from the top right corner of your iPhone screen
- You will see a variety of symbols and controls. Locate the "**Screen Recording**" button, which appears as a solid circle inside a circle.
- In the Control Center, press the "**Screen Recording**" button.
- A three-second countdown timer will show, allowing you time to prepare.
- Following the countdown, your iPhone screen will begin recording. The recording is in progress, as indicated by a red status bar at the top of the screen.

Customize the Recording Audio Settings (Optional)

- Force touch (push forcefully) the "**Screen Recording**" button in the Control Center to open further recording options.
- A pop-up menu will display, enabling you to turn on or off microphone audio for your recording. You can also allow or disable the display of touches on the screen.
- Proceed to tailor the settings to your preferences.

End the Recording

- Tap the red status bar at the top of your iPhone screen to stop recording.
- Alternatively, you can reopen the Control Center and stop the recording by tapping the "**Screen Recording**" icon.
- When you finish recording, a notice will appear informing you that your video has been saved to your Photos app.
- Launch the Photos app and look for your recorded video in the "**Recents**" album or the "**Videos**" folder.

Frequently Asked Questions

1. How do you record in ProRAW on your iPhone 15 Series?
2. How do you record ProRes on your iPhone 15 Series?
3. What are the best iPhone 15 Pro and Pro Max accessories for filmmaking?
4. How do you record cinematic videos?
5. How do you adjust cinematic mode focus post-shoot?
6. How do you trim a video?
7. How do you cut a clip out of a video?
8. How do you record your iPhone screen?

CHAPTER FOUR
PHOTOGRAPHIC STYLES, EXPOSURE, AND OTHER CAMERA SETTINGS

Overview

Chapter four talks about Photographic styles, how to adjust exposure, and other camera settings including the camera flash and others.

What exactly are photographic styles?

Photographic Styles are not filters; rather, they are camera app preset settings for Tone and Warmth that allow you to modify what your iPhone camera records in real-time. The default Photographic Style is always Standard, which provides an overall balanced appearance. However, there are four alternative options: Rich Contrast, Vibrant, Warm, and Cool. In the Settings app, you can change the default to a different setting so that it always starts on that choice, or you may move between them all while shooting in the Camera app. Furthermore, although each preset has its default Tone and Warmth settings, you can further tweak them to your satisfaction if you choose. This allows you to develop your own "**style**" with each shot you take. Photographic Styles, on the other hand, cannot be added after the fact, thus they are not filters. They're also considered destructive since you can't alter the Photographic Style of a picture after it's been recorded; if you want to switch to a different style, you'll have to shoot the photo again in real-time with that style applied.

Why are photographic styles so appealing?

Though the Standard option is typically enough for ordinary images, most people are not always pleased with how iOS handles color processing after shooting. Since the Standard option has a "**balanced**" approach, some people believe certain components of a photograph seem washed out. However, Photographic Styles help to reduce this problem. Rich Contrast, which offers deeper shadows and richer colors for great contrast in a shot, is the favorite of the six presets. However, Vibrant is also useful if you want to get brighter and more vibrant colors while maintaining a balanced appearance. Warm enhances the golden undertones, while Cool enhances the blue undertones.

How to Set up Photographic Styles

If you're interested in Photographic Styles and want to test them out for yourself, there are two options.

Create a standard photographic style

Everyone has the Standard style enabled by default. You can, however, change it to one of the other presets so that it is always ready to go whenever you access the Camera app.

1. Open the Settings app on your iPhone (iPhone 13 or later required).
2. Scroll down and click on **Camera**.
3. Choose **Photographic Styles**.
4. Swipe between the various styles: Standard (default), Rich Contrast, Vibrant, Warm, and Cool.
5. Choose "**Use** "**Style**" for the one you desire.

When you activate the Camera app, it will now begin with the one you choose. However, if you modify the style in the following stage, your option will be overridden.

Create a Photographic Style in the Camera app

You can also use the Camera app to flip between all of the preset presets.

Here's how it's done:

1. Open the **Camera app** on your iPhone (iPhone 13 or later, such as the iPhone 15 Series).
2. Swipe up from the viewfinder's bottom (the area above the shutter button). To access the extra controls, press the arrow at the top of the screen.
3. Choose the Photographic Styles option. It seems to be three overlapping squares.
4. Swipe through the many styles, including Standard, Rich Contrast, Vibrant, Warm, and Cool.
5. If you want to change the tone or warmth of each style, use the sliders.

Remember that, although you may choose between them in the Camera app, any style you leave on becomes the default, even overriding what you initially selected in the Settings app.

How to turn the camera flash on or off

If you follow the steps below, you can switch on the flash on the iPhone 15 and have it operate every time you snap a shot.

The steps:

1. Swipe up on the **Camera viewfinder area** in the Camera app.
2. From the button menu, choose the **flash button** to get the Auto, On, and Off flash options.
3. Choose the **'On'** option so that Flash On displays on the screen.

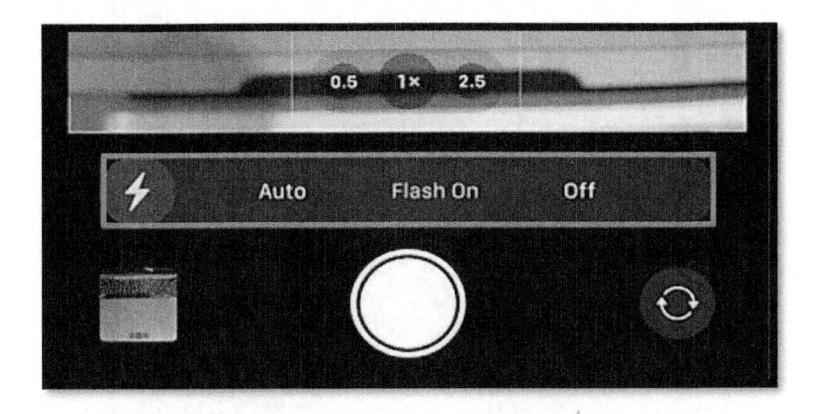

- Now that you've turned on the flash, the flash button in the upper left corner should become yellow. This means that regardless of the lighting conditions, your iPhone 15's camera flash will activate whenever you capture a shot or begin recording a video.
- If you don't want the flash to turn on every time, you can set it to **'Auto'** or **'Off'**.
- You can also quickly turn off the flash by tapping on the **yellow flash button**.

How to adjust focus and exposure

Here are the steps to follow to adjust focus and exposure:

- After unlocking your iPhone, look for the Camera app on the home screens. Tap on the camera to open it.

- Change the focus manually by touching the relevant area of the screen. As a consequence, the area you touched will have a yellow square or circle around it to indicate that the camera's attention has shifted to that position.

- After you've touched the screen to set the focal point, modify the exposure. A sun symbol should be placed adjacent to the focus box.
- You can adjust the exposure using the slider to the right of the focus point. Swipe up to increase exposure and down to decrease exposure to brighten or darken a photo.

- Touch and hold the screen until the AE/AF Lock notice shows to lock both exposure and focus. This ensures that even if the scene changes, the camera will preserve the focus and exposure settings you've selected.
- To return to automatic focus and exposure, just tap a different section of the screen.
- Look for a white balance icon or option in your camera app. This is commonly represented with a sun-shaped symbol. To adjust the white balance, move the slider to the left or right.

How to use a timer

The camera app on the iPhone 15 Series, like previous iPhones, enables users to snap a timed shot. Setting a time delay on the iPhone 15 camera is useful for hands-free shooting and comes in handy in a variety of circumstances. You can, for example, use a delay to obtain long-exposure shots of moving scenes such as light trails or waterfalls. The 10-second delay timer allows you to take a group shot while your iPhone is on a tripod. You can also snap high-quality selfies with the back camera and obtain better macro and low-light images by using the camera timer. Set a timer on the iPhone 14 camera to capture significantly better images since the self or camera timer minimizes shaking. Within the iPhone's native camera app, you can choose a 3-second or 10-second timer.

Here are the steps:

1. Switch to **Photo or Portrait mode** in the Camera app.
2. Swipe up on the viewfinder or tap the up arrow symbol at the top center of the screen.

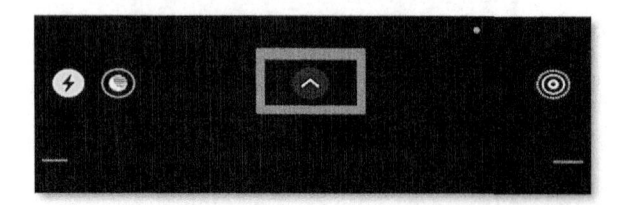

3. Right above the shutter button, a toolbar with circular icons will now emerge.
4. Select the timer icon. If you don't see the timer, swipe the icons row to the left.

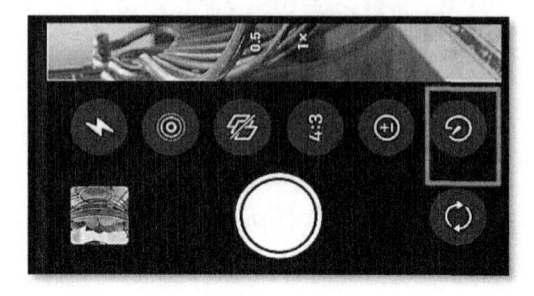

5. Timer Off is the default setting from here. You have the option of using a 3-second or 10-second timer. Select the desired option.

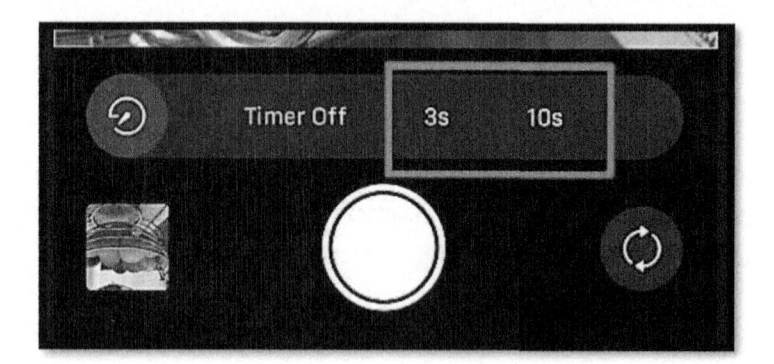

6. To confirm, the symbol will become yellow, and the countdown timer length will be shown at the top.

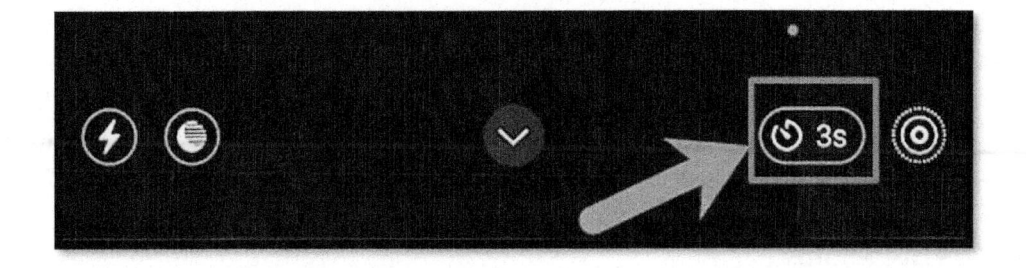

7. To snap a shot with a timer on your iPhone, press the shutter or volume button.
8. Since the setting is only saved for a limited period, remember to activate the camera timer anytime you wish to snap a timed shot on iPhone 15.

How can I disable the timer on my iPhone 15 camera?

Looking to disable seconds or delete the iPhone camera's 3-second delay?

- To disable the timer, go to the **Camera app's Timer option** and toggle it to Off.

How does the iPhone camera timer work?

When you set a delay timer (3s or 10s) and push the shutter button, a countdown timer shows on the screen before the camera takes a shot automatically. The camera flashlight blinks every second to indicate the countdown. When using the timing option, the iPhone takes a burst shot of ten photographs rather than a single snapshot. You can also set a photo timer on the iPhone 15 for both the front and back cameras.

Tips for Using the Timer on an iPhone to Take Photos

The tips include the following:

- **Use a tripod**

While you can support the phone up against anything or use a kickstand, using a tripod may result in better images. If so, keep it at eye level, but you may also get creative with angles, particularly for group shots, such as snapping them from above. A tripod, on the other hand, is perfect for capturing night shots since it helps to eliminate blur produced by shakiness. Although the newest iPhones have capabilities to fight this, it's still worth using a tripod.

- **Position the iPhone in the right way**

It is particularly vital to position the phone appropriately while shooting images outside. If you're shooting them during the day, angle the camera so that the sun is behind it or off to the side to minimize glare.

- **Use Live Photos**

Use the Live Photos function, which will automatically record 1.5 seconds before and 1.5 seconds after the picture was captured, especially when taking group or action photos. This way, you may go back and forth to find the precise frame you want. However, keep in mind that Live Photos consume significantly more space on the phone than a single photo.

- **Keep Burst Mode enabled**

Did you know that when you snap a shot with the timer on your iPhone (assuming you have Live Photos turned off), Burst Mode is on by default? If you prefer this over Live photographs, keep it turned on, and you'll receive 10 photographs taken every time you press the shutter. Burst (10 images) will appear at the top of the shot, and you may browse through to choose and save just the one you wish. This eliminates the need for everyone to pose many times for the same photo, or for you to hit the timer button more than once to capture multiple images.

How to set a timer on iPhone 15 without Burst?

The timer's Burst mode is useful since it allows you to choose the best photograph from 10 burst images. Simultaneously, you wind up shooting many shots of the same subject even when you don't need them. When using the timer, there is no option to deactivate Burst mode. However, there is an easy workaround for turning off burst mode on the self-timer. To use the camera timer on iPhone 15 without Burst, go to Live Photo or Portrait mode, or turn on the flash. Take a shot with the timer on, and the Burst mode will not activate.

How to take a photo with a filter

Pre-loaded iPhone filters will give your images a creative touch without requiring you to download additional applications. These are great for quick modifications when you don't need to go beyond what's pre-set in the basic filters. The iPhone Camera app has 9 pre-installed filters to enhance your images. You can get a live preview of the filters while shooting a photograph in the Camera app, or you can check the filter effects on a previously shot photo in the Photos app.

How to use the iPhone camera app to capture a shot with a filter

To add filters to any iPhone running iOS 17, follow the steps below:

1. Launch the **Camera app**.
2. Tap the up arrow at the top of the screen after selecting either Photo or Portrait mode. Near the bottom of the screen, a black bar with 5 icons will emerge. At the far right, tap the symbol with three crossing circles.
3. A slider will appear with brief previews of the filters. Swipe between the filters to see their names and a live preview.
4. After you've chosen your filter, take a photo by tapping the Shutter button underneath the slider.

How to add a filter to a photo you've already taken

Here are the steps:

1. Launch the **Photos app**.
2. Scroll through your picture collection, choose one to modify, and tap it.
3. Tap **Edit** in the upper right corner of the screen.
4. Tap the **Filter icon** (three overlapping circles) at the bottom of the screen.
5. A slider will appear with brief previews of the filters. Swipe between the filters to see their names and a live preview.
6. Tap **Done** to apply your filter.
7. Tap **Cancel** to delete your filter and other changes.

Default photo filters and how they transform photos

Using one of the iPhone's 9 free photo filters can give your shot a cool blue temperature or a dramatic noir effect for a vintage vibe.

Here's a short rundown of each filter:

- **Vibrant**: Increases contrast.
- **Vivid Warm**: Adds a yellow hue to the vivid filter.

- **Vivid Cool**: Adds a blue tint to the vivid filter.
- **Dramatic**: Increases the shadows and decreases the highlights.
- **Dramatic Warm**: Adds a yellow hue to the Dramatic filter.
- **Dramatic Cool**: Apply a blue tint to the Dramatic filter.
- **Mono**: Converts to plain black and white.
- **Silvertone**: Becomes black and white with greater shadows.
- **Noir**: Converts to black and white with a strong contrast.

How to align your photo using a grid

Do you want to correct the horizon in a photo? Or maybe you're curious about how to capture more interesting images. Gridlines can be enabled to appear in your Camera app in both circumstances, enabling you to create level shots while also using the oh-so-powerful rule of thirds for stunning photo compositions. Setting faint gridlines to appear in your Camera app will help you shoot more level photographs, use the rule of thirds, **and eliminate unnecessary editing processes like cropping. More on the rule of thirds follows, but for now, here's how to create a grid to appear in your iPhone Camera app:**

1. Launch the **Settings app**.
2. Select **Camera**.

3. Locate the **Grid** and turn it on.

4. Move back to the Camera app; a faint grid will appear across the capture frame.

After activating the iPhone camera grid, you can begin learning how to build balanced compositions that follow the rule of thirds.

Using the Rule of Thirds in Your iPhone Photos

There are no hard and fast laws in life. However, if you're new to photography, knowing the rule of thirds may assist you with the overall balance and mood of your photos.

On your iPhone, the rule of thirds operates as follows:

- The camera grid is divided into nine equal-sized squares.
- According to the rule of thirds, the major compositional components or themes should be located along the lines or at the intersections of the lines.
- The horizon line (of your picture) should also align with the grid's top or bottom horizontal line.

The rule of thirds is a very basic photographic guideline, yet it makes a huge impact. The iPhone camera is getting closer to professional DSLR cameras. While an iPhone camera can never completely replace a professional camera, knowing a few fundamental photography concepts may improve your ordinary photographs to a level worthy of Instagram stardom.

Frequently Asked Questions

1. How do you choose a photographic style?
2. How do you set up Photographic styles?
3. How do you turn the camera flash on or off?
4. How do you adjust focus and exposure?
5. How do you use a timer on your iPhone 15 Series?
6. How do you take a photo using a filter?
7. How do you align your image using a grid?

CHAPTER FIVE
PHOTOS APP

Overview

What is there to talk about the iPhone 15 Series camera without discussing the Photos app where the magic happens? Chapter five discusses the Photos app and how you can use it efficiently

How to navigate through the Photos app

View photos and videos in the Photos app on the iPhone

To discover and see all of the photos and videos on your iPhone, use the photos app.

How photos and videos are organized in Photos

At the bottom of the screen, you may browse Photos by using the Library, For You, Albums, and Search buttons.

- **Library**: Search through your photos and videos by days, months, years, or all images.
- **For You**: A customized feed displays your memories, shared images, and highlighted photos.
- **Albums**: View albums you've made or shared, as well as photographs automatically categorized by categories such as People and pets, Places, and Media Types.
- **Search**: Enter a search term into the search bar to find images based on their date, location, caption, or the things they include. Alternatively, you may explore photos that have already been organized by significant events, people, locations, and subjects.

Browse photos in your library

Tap Library, and then pick any of the following to view your photos and videos by when they were taken:

- **Years**: Find a certain year in your picture collection quickly.
- **Months**: View collections of images you shot over a month, categorized by major events such as a family excursion, social gathering, birthday celebration, or travel.
- **Days**: View your greatest images in chronological sequence, organized by the time or location in which they were shot.
- **All Photos:** Browse through all of your photographs and videos.

Pinch the screen to zoom in or out while viewing All Photos. You can also zoom in and out, browse photos by aspect ratio or square, filter photos, and display photos on a map by tapping . Years, Months, and Days views are selected to present your greatest images while excluding visual clutter such as similar photographs, screenshots, whiteboards, and receipts. Tap All Photos to view every photo and video.

View individual images

- On your iPhone, tap a picture to see it in full-screen mode.
- To zoom in on the picture, double-tap or pinch out—drag to view various portions of the shot; to zoom out, double-tap or pinch closed.
- Tap ♡ to save the image to your Favorites album.
- Touch and hold the picture to play it while viewing a Live Photo.
- To continue exploring or return to the search results, tap ＜ or drag the picture down.

See photo and video information

Open a picture or video to see stored metadata information, then touch ⓘ or slide up. You will observe the following information depending on the picture or video:

- Individuals are recognized in the photo.
- A caption field to explain the picture or video and make it more easily found in Search.
- Items discovered using Visual Look Up.
- Whether the picture was sent to you via Messages, another app, or the iCloud Shared picture Library.

- The time and date the picture or video was captured; tap **Adjust** to change the time and date.
- Metadata from the camera, such as the lens, shutter speed, file size, and so on.
- The location of the picture or video; press the link to examine the location in Maps; hit **Adjust** to change the location.

How to Delete and Share Photos

Delete

If you have a large number of images on your iPhone, it may be slowing it down. Furthermore, although your iPhone comes with a free iCloud account, it only provides 5GB of storage, which may not be enough for all of your images and movies. If you need to free up some space, here's how to rapidly erase all of your images from your iPhone and how to delete all of your iCloud photos. To erase all of your iPhone's images, launch the images app and go to **Photos > All Photos**. Then, press the last picture and drag up until all photos and videos are chosen. Finally, choose **Delete Photos** from the **Trash button**.

The steps:

1. On your iPhone, launch the **Photos app**.
2. Then choose **Library**. This will appear in the bottom-left corner of your screen.

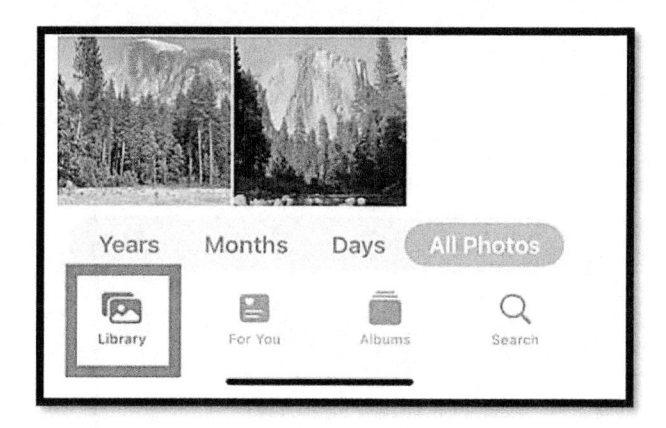

3. Then, choose **All Photos**. This will appear in the lower-right corner of your screen.

4. Tap the **Select button**. This will appear in the upper-right corner of your screen.
5. Then, tap the last photo carefully and move your finger to the top of your screen. If you push too hard, you will instead get a preview of the shot. Drag your finger horizontally over the first picture and then up to the top of your screen for the best results.

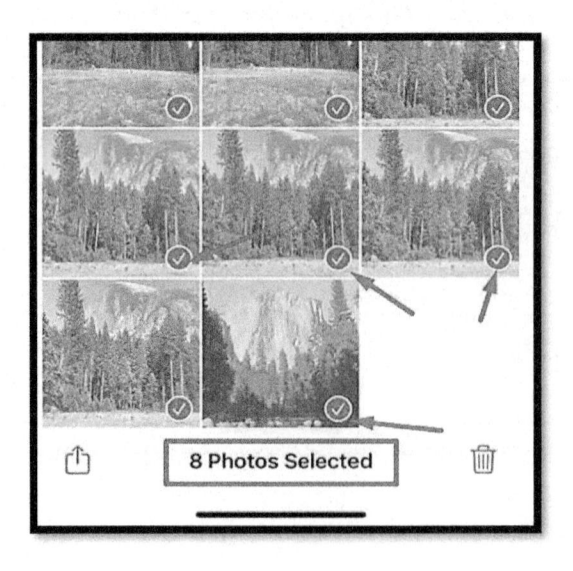

6. Then choose the **Trash icon**. This can be found in the bottom-right corner of your screen.

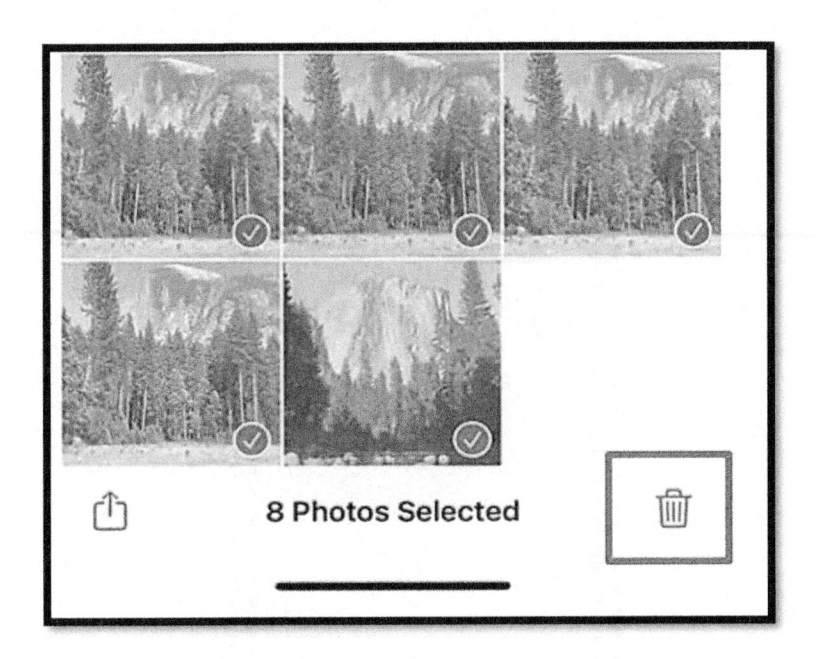

7. Then tap the **Delete Photos button**. This will display the number of photos you are removing. When you have erased all of your photographs, the words No photographs or Videos will appear in the center of the screen.

Unless you delete them manually, it might take up to 30 days for all of your images to be erased from your iPhone. To do so, go to Albums and then scroll down to Recently Deleted. Then, tap **Select > Delete All**. Also, tap the **Delete Photos button**. This action cannot be reversed.

Share

Share photos and videos on iPhone

Photos and videos from the Photos app can be shared in Mail, Messages, and other applications you install. By bringing one iPhone near to another, you can easily exchange photos and videos.

The steps:

- To share a single image or video, open it, tap ⬆, and then choose a sharing option such as Mail, Messages, or AirDrop.

- When you're viewing a screen with numerous thumbnails, press **Select**, then select the thumbnail of the photos and videos you want to share. Tap ⬆️ and then choose a sharing method such as Mail, Messages, or AirDrop.

- To share photos or videos from a certain day or month, go to Library, Days or Months, tap 😀, then **Share photos**, and choose a sharing method such as Mail, Messages, or AirDrop.

When you enable iCloud photos, you can share numerous full-quality photographs using an iCloud link. iCloud links are viewable by everyone and may be shared using any app, like Messages or Mail, for 30 days. Shared Albums can also be used to share photographs and videos with just the individuals you choose. Keep in mind that the size of attachments is regulated by your service provider. A Live snapshot is sent as a still snapshot for devices or services that do not support Live Photos.

Adjust the sharing options

You can change the format; file type, and information that is sent with a picture or video before sharing it.

1. **Open the picture or video, touch, ⬆️ hit Options, and then choose one of the following options:**
- To disable location data, tap the button next to Location (green is turned on).
- **Change the file format**: Select Automatic for the optimum file format for the destination, Current to avoid a file format conversion, or Most Compatible to convert files to .JPG or. MOV.
- **Send as iCloud link**: Tap the green button next to iCloud Link to send a URL to view or download the photos or videos. For 30 days, iCloud connections are accessible.
- **Send all photo data:** Tap the button next to All Photos Data (green is on) to send the original file with edit history and metadata; the receiver may examine the current version and alter modifications (only AirDrop and iCloud links are accessible).
2. Select **Done**.

Share photos and videos by bringing one iPhone close to another

Simply putting the two iPhones close enough allows you to transfer photos and videos from one to the other.

1. Check that each iPhone is turned on, unlocked, and has AirDrop enabled.

2. Check that the sender and recipient are both contacts in each other's Contacts apps.
3. Open the Photos app on your iPhone with the objects you want to share, then perform one of the following:
   - **Share a single picture or video**: Open the photo or video you want to share and hold it in the center of the screen.
   - **Share multiple images or videos:** Select, and then tap numerous photos or videos from your collection to share.
4. Connect the devices, and then hit **Share**. The items shared are saved in the recipient's Photos library.

Save or share a photo or video you receive

The steps:

- **From an email**: If required, tap to download the item, then tap ⬆. Alternatively, tap and hold the object before selecting a sharing or saving option.

- **From a text message**, tap the picture or video in the conversation, then touch ⬆ and choose a sharing or storing option. You can also save the picture or video straight to your Photos library by tapping ⬆ in the Messages chat.

- **From an iCloud link**: Tap ⬆ the collection in the Messages discussion to save it straight to your Photos library. To share the collection, open Photos, go to For You, and then to iCloud Links. Tap ⋯ and then Share.

Import and Export Videos

Import and export photos and videos on iPhone

You can easily import photographs and videos from a digital camera, an SD memory card, or another iPhone with a camera into the photographs app. You can also save unaltered copies of your images and movies to an external disk, memory card, or other storage device linked to your iPhone.

Import photos and videos to your iPhone

Import photos and videos from another device, such as a digital camera or an external drive, into your iPhone's photos app.

92

The steps:

1. Connect the camera adapter or card reader to the USB-C port on your iPhone, or connect it directly to the device.
2. **Perform one of the following:**
- **Connect a camera**: Plug in the adapter, then turn on the camera and ensure it is in transfer mode. More information may be found in the camera's documentation.
- Insert an SD memory card or connect an external storage device into the card reader: Do not push the card into the slot on the reader; it fits only one way.
- **Connect an iPhone:** Connect the device to the camera adapter using the USB-C cable that comes with it. Turn the smartphone on and unlock it.
3. Open your iPhone's Photos app, then hit **Import**.
4. Choose the photos and videos you want to import, then choose an import location.
- To import all products, choose **Import All**.
- **Import selected items**: Choose the things to import (a check mark appears for each), press Import, and then choose Import chosen.
5. Keep or delete the imported photos and videos from the camera, card, iPhone, or iPad.
6. Remove the camera adapter or card reader from the system.

Export photos and videos to an external storage device

You can easily export images and movies taken on your iPhone to an external disk, memory card, or other storage device. For edited photos and videos, the unaltered original form will be exported.

The steps:

1. Connect the storage device to your iPhone using the USB-C connection, or connect the device directly to your iPhone.
2. Select the photos and videos you want to export in the photos app.
3. Tap ⬆ then choose **Export Unmodified Original**.
4. Tap your storage device (under Locations), then **Save**.

Share long videos on your iPhone

Long films recorded with your iPhone camera may be sent by AirDrop, iCloud, or Mail Drop from the Photos app.

Use AirDrop to send a video

You can use AirDrop to transfer a huge movie to a nearby iPhone, iPad, or Mac. AirDrop delivers data over Wi-Fi and Bluetooth, so make sure both you and the receiver have these controls enabled in the Control Center before sharing. **Here are the steps:**

1. If the individual to whom you're sending the video isn't already in your contacts, have them perform one of the following:
   - On an iPhone or iPad, go to **Settings > General > AirDrop**, then tap **everyone for 10 Minutes**.
   - On a Mac, direct them to the **Apple menu > System Preferences > General > AirDrop & Handoff**, and then choose **everyone**.
2. Open your photo library, then select the video you want to share and tap ⬆️. Tap Options, then choose **All Photos Data** to share the movie in its original format, including metadata, location, and any related modification history or subtitles.
3. Tap AirDrop, and then tap the person or device with whom you want to share. After you share, the receiver is notified and given the option to accept or deny the AirDrop transmission.

Send a video using an iCloud link

An iCloud link is a URL that allows you to transfer a big movie over Messages or Mail. **Make sure iCloud Photos is enabled before sending an iCloud link. Then take the following steps:**

1. Open your photo library, and then press the video you want to share and tap ⬆️.
2. Tap Options, then iCloud Link, and finally **Done**.
3. Tap Messages or Mail, input the iCloud link's recipient, and then tap ⬆️ to send the message or email. You have 30 days to download the video delivered with an iCloud link.

Send a video using Mail Drop

You can use Mail Drop to send a huge movie as an attachment in Mail. **Here are the steps:**

1. Open your photo library, and then choose the video you would like to send.
2. Tap ⬆️ and then **Mail**.
3. Enter the recipient's name or email address in the To box. Tap the subject area or email body to add a subject or message.
4. To send, just tap ⬆️. Mail Drop attachments can be downloaded for 30 days by recipients.

How to add text to your pictures

Using Apple's Photos app

The iOS Photos app's Markup function allows you to add text to images and screenshots. You may use whatever color you like, choose a font size, and choose one of three font styles. **Here's how to easily add text to a photo on your iPhone:**

1. Open the **Photos app** and choose the image to which you want to add text.
2. Select **Edit**.

3. Hit the plus (+) button and pick **Text** as well.
4. Precede to double-tap the "**Text**" box and start typing. Tap anywhere on the image to hide the on-screen keyboard.
5. Tap to pick your text. Tap **AA** to change the font style, size, and alignment. Next, choose a color from the color palette or press the color palette dot to use a custom color and adjust the opacity. You can also hit the color picker icon in the upper left corner and drag it over the picture to choose a color that fits that section of the image.
6. Drag the text to the correct location on the picture and hit **Done**. The text has now been added to your image. It can be sent over iMessage or shared on Instagram, Twitter, Facebook, WhatsApp Stories, and other social media sites.

Using Phonto

Phonto is a highly-rated free app that allows you to easily add text to images in a variety of styles.

1. Install and launch the Phonto app on your iPhone.
2. From the bottom, tap the camera symbol and then choose Photo Albums. After that, grant the app access to your photo collection.

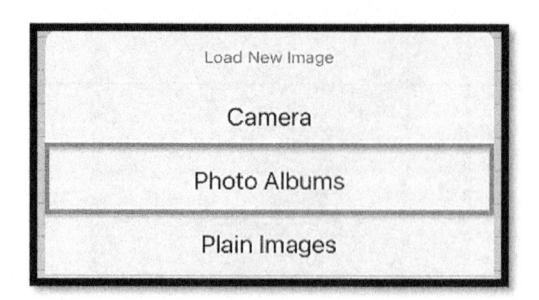

3. Select the picture on which you want to add text.
4. Click **Done** to close the filter panel.
5. Once in the main editor, press anywhere on the picture and choose **Add Text**.

6. Enter your message, and then choose from a variety of font styles and symbols. You can also choose between left, right, or center alignment. You may also change the wording to today's date by selecting Preset. You may modify these defaults to custom text later in the app's settings section. Once you've finished everything here, tap **Done**.
7. Drag the text to the desired location on the picture. You may also choose an option from the resulting sub-menu. What they do is as follows:

- **Text**: This will return you to the text-input screen from Step 6.
- **Style**: Text color, stroke (text border), background, shadow, spacing, underlining, and blend are all choices. It will take some time to adjust to everything here. Remember to use the top-level Color and Style tabs.
- **Font**: Choose a font.
- **Size**: Change the size of the text.
- **Tilt**: Select a tilt angle for your picture.
- **Move**: To accurately move the text, use the four arrow buttons.
- **Curve**: Make the text curve inwards or outwards.

8. After you've added text to the picture, hit the **share button** and choose **Save Image or Save Image as PNG**. After that, open the Photos app on your iPhone or iPad to discover the finished altered image.

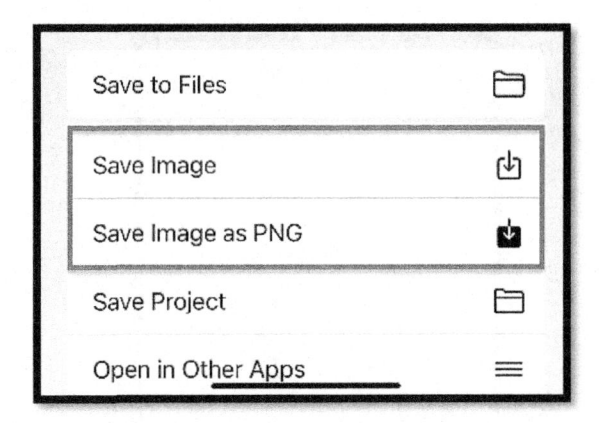

How to Recover Deleted Pictures and Videos from the Photos App

Taking images using your iPhone 15's built-in camera is relatively simple in this age of smartphone photography. The same is true when you choose to delete. A simple swipe on the screen can erase a picture from your photo gallery that you don't want to save.

However, there is a potential that you may remove images that are important to you. It might be inconvenient if you mistakenly erase a picture from your iPhone 15. However, there are a few steps you can follow to avoid difficulties and recover irreversibly lost images on your iPhone 15, even if you believe they are unrecoverable.

Is it possible to restore lost images from an iPhone 15?

When a picture is transferred to the Recently Deleted folder in the Photos app within the last 30 days, iPhone 15 owners can easily restore it. However, if you want to recover irreversibly lost images from iPhone 15 and you can't locate them in that specific folder, you may have to depend on your phone backups. There are also several third-party iPhone recovery software tools available to scan your iPhone 14 for lost images. Remember that recovering iPhone 15 to retrieve deleted images from backup—whether in iCloud or on your PC or Mac—is only possible if you backed up the device before your photos were erased. **Here are the steps:**

1. Unlock your iPhone and use the Photos app to access your photo collection. Your images are organized into four groups: **"My Albums," "People & Places," "Media Types," and "Utilities."**
2. Scroll to the bottom of the screen until you see **"Utilities**," then touch **"Recently Deleted."**

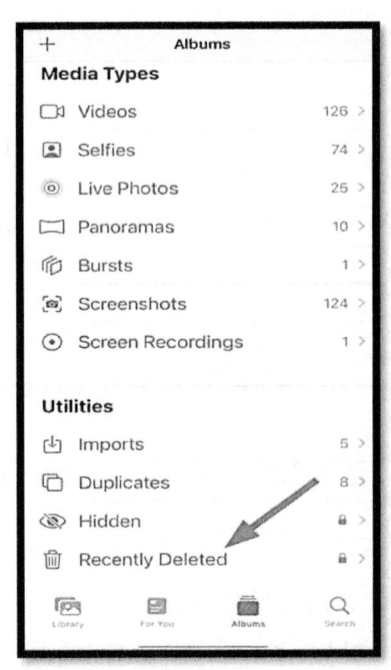

3. Unlock the "**Recently Deleted**" album using your Face ID.
4. It will display a list of images you recently erased, as well as the amount of days before they are permanently wiped from your iPhone 15. iOS reminds you at the bottom of the screen that the images (and videos) will be saved for up to 40 days. You can retrieve the photographs during this time.

5. In the top right corner of the screen, tap **Select**.
6. Select the deleted photos from the screen that you want to recover, and then select "**Recover**" in the lower right corner. It will ask you how many photos you want to restore.

7. Tap "**Recover [Number] Photos**" to confirm in the pop-up to recover your deleted images.

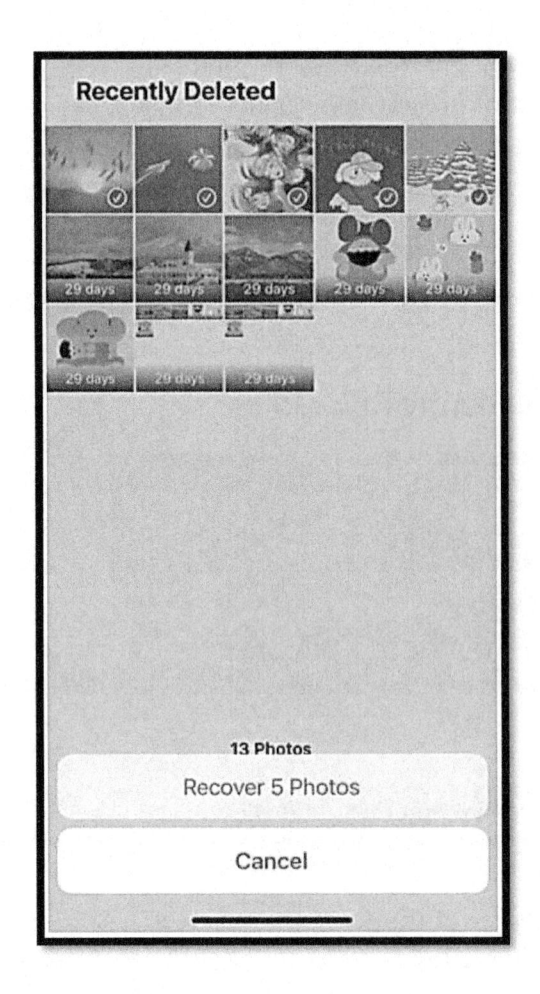

You can't use the "**Recently Deleted**" function in the iPhone 15 Photos app to retrieve a picture that was deleted more than 30 days ago. Fortunately, there is a workaround: you can use a specialist picture recovery tool of your choosing to recover lost images from the iPhone 15's memory without using a backup.

How to make a photo part of your favorite

When you like a picture, it is preserved/saved in the Favorites album.

1. Launch the **Photos app**.
2. Tap the heart symbol at the bottom of the screen and choose one of your favorite photos or videos.
3. The heart symbol will change to blue, indicating that your photo has been saved to Favorites.

4. To access your favorites, go to the **Albums tab** and then to Favorites.

5. To delete a photo from your favorite album, open it by tapping on it.
6. Tap the heart once more. When the heart is no longer blue, the image is no longer in Favorites.
7. Deleting a picture from your Favorites album does not delete it from All Photos. If you want to completely erase a photo from your Photo Library, don't hit the trash can symbol next to the love icon.

How to hide photos and videos and access them

The option to hide images and videos in a different folder so that they are not visible while browsing through the main albums is a major privacy feature on iPhones. Apple has long emphasized iOS's privacy features as part of its attempts to distinguish its smartphone platform from Android. Apple also included several new privacy features with iOS 16 and 17, including a **'Safety Check'** function that can be used to reset the data and location access allowed to others. Another new privacy feature is **'Emergency Reset,'** which prevents any data exchange with other persons or applications. The native photos app is the easiest method to hide photographs on your iPhone, iPad, or iPod Touch. It removes the chosen photos from your main library and search results. Hidden photos are relocated to a Hidden album, which may be accessed on the Albums page and in the Utilities section. Furthermore, you can only see your Hidden album after unlocking it with Face ID or your device's PIN code.

Here are the steps:

- On your iPhone, launch the **Photos app**.
- Locate the photos you want to hide.
- Tap on each picture you want to hide.
- Tap the **Overflow symbol** in the lower-right corner. It seems to be (...).
- Click the **Hide button**.

- The selected photos will now be moved to the Hidden album, which can be found on the Albums page under Utilities.

How to unhide or view hidden photos

It's as simple as going to the Album page and scrolling down to see or unhides hidden photos.

Here's how:

1. Open the **Photos app**.
2. At the bottom, tap the **Albums tab**.
3. Scroll down and hit the Utilities folder's Hidden folder. At this point, you'll be prompted to activate Face ID access.

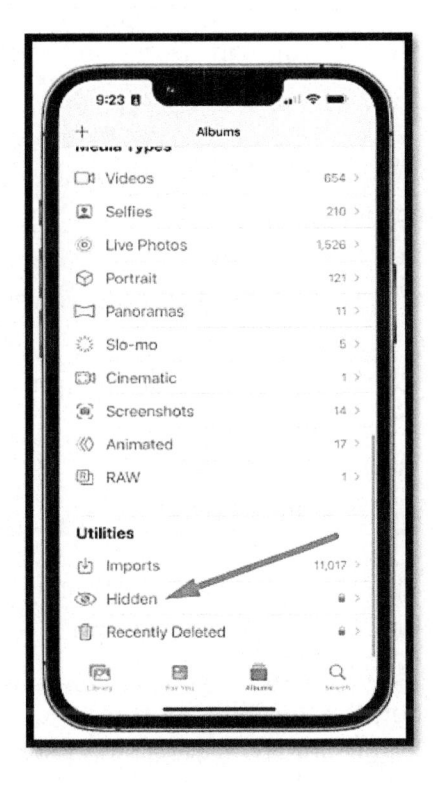

4. Tap the **Select button** in the upper-right corner.
5. Tap on each picture you want to unhide.
6. In the bottom-left corner, tap the **Overflow button**. As previously, it looks like an ellipsis surrounded by a circle.

7. On the pop-up menu, choose **Unhide**. The photos will subsequently be returned to their original locations. Alternatively, you can add them to an album by tapping Add to album.

How to crop, flip, and rotate photos

Cropping photos

- On your iPhone 15 Series, launch the **Photos app**.
- Choose the picture to be cropped.
- In the upper right corner, tap the "**Edit**" button.
- At the bottom of the screen, you'll see a collection of editing tools. Select the "**Crop**" tool (it resembles a square with diagonal lines).
- Resize and adjust the cropping frame with your fingertips to the appropriate location.
- When you're happy with the crop, tap "**Done**" in the bottom-right corner.

Flipping Photos

- On your iPhone 15 Series, launch the **Photos app**.
- Choose the picture to be flipped.
- In the upper right corner, tap the "**Edit**" button.
- Tap the "**Adjustments**" tool (it looks like a dial or slider) at the bottom of the screen.
- Look for a feature that lets you flip or rotate the image horizontally or vertically. This can be called "**Flip**" or "**Mirror**."
- Adjust the flip or mirror as required.
- When you're done, tap the "**Done**" button.

Rotating Photos

- On your iPhone 15 Series, launch the **Photos app**.
- Choose the picture to be rotated.
- In the upper right corner, tap the "**Edit**" button.
- At the bottom of the screen, you'll see a collection of editing tools. The "**Crop**" tool (a square with diagonal lines) is selected.
- To rotate the picture, twist it with your fingers to the appropriate orientation.
- You can rotate the picture by touching the rotation controls (typically curving arrows) until it's in the correct position.
- When you're finished with the rotation, tap the "**Done**" button.

How to change the lighting and color scheme

Adjust the screen brightness and color on the iPhone

You can dim or brighten your iPhone's screen (dimming the screen increases battery life). You may also manually or automatically modify the screen brightness and color using Dark Mode, True Tone, and Night Shift.

Manually adjust the screen brightness

Do one of the following to dim or brighten your iPhone's screen:

- Launch **Control Center** and then drag up or down.
- Navigate to **Settings > Display & Brightness** and move the slider.

Automatically adjust the screen brightness

Using the built-in ambient light sensor, the iPhone changes the screen brightness based on the current lighting conditions.

Here are the steps:

1. Navigate to the **Settings > Accessibility menu**.
2. Select **Display & Text Size**, then **Auto-Brightness**.

Turn Dark Mode on or off

Dark Mode transforms the whole iPhone experience into a dark color scheme that is ideal for low-light situations. With Dark Mode enabled, you may use your iPhone while reading in bed, for example, without disturbing the person next to you.

Perform any of the following:

- Open Control Center, then touch and hold and tap to toggle Dark Mode on or off.
- Go to **Settings > Display & Brightness**, then pick **Dark** to enable Dark Mode or **Light** to disable it.

Schedule Dark Mode to turn on and off automatically

In Settings, you can configure Dark Mode to activate automatically at night (or on a custom schedule).

Here are the steps:

1. Navigate to **Settings > Display** and **Brightness**.
2. Select **Automatic**, then **Options**.
3. Choose from **Sunset to Sunrise** and Custom Schedule.

If you choose Custom arrange, you can arrange when you want Dark Mode to switch on and off. When you choose Sunset to Sunrise, your iPhone uses your clock and geolocation to calculate when it is evening for you.

Turn the Night Shift on or off

You can manually activate Night Shift, which is useful when you're in a gloomy room during the day.

- Launch Control Center, then touch and hold ☼, then tap ☾.

Schedule the Night Shift to turn on and off automatically

Schedule Night changes to change the colors in your display to the warmer end of the spectrum at night, making it easier for your eyes to see the screen.

Follow the steps below:

1. Select **Display & Brightness > Night Shift** from the menu.
2. Enable **Scheduled**.
3. Drag the slider underneath Color Temperature toward the warmer or cooler end of the spectrum to modify the color balance for Night Shift.
4. Select **Sunset to Sunrise or Custom Schedule** from the menu.

If you choose Custom set, use the choices to set when Night Shift will switch on and off. When you choose Sunset to Sunrise, your iPhone uses your clock and geolocation to calculate when it is evening for you. If you switch off Location Services in **Settings > Privacy & Security or Setting Time Zone** in **Settings > Privacy & Security > Location Services > System Services**, the Sunset to Sunrise option will be unavailable.

Turn True Tone on or off

True Tone automatically adjusts the display's hue and intensity to fit the light in your area.

Perform any of the following:

- Open Control Center, then touch and hold ☼ and tap ☰ to toggle True Tone on or off.
- Navigate to **Settings > Display & Brightness** and toggle True Tone on or off.

How to revert an adjusted image

Do you want to restore a picture to its original state? If you mistakenly over-edited an otherwise fantastic photo in the Photos app and then saved it, don't worry. This trick will enable you to restore the original picture as if the edits never occurred.

Follow the steps below to do so:

1. Launch the **Photos app**.
2. Find the picture that you want to restore to its original state.

3. Tap the **Edit button** in the upper right corner of the picture you want to revert to.

4. Tap **Revert** at the bottom of your screen.

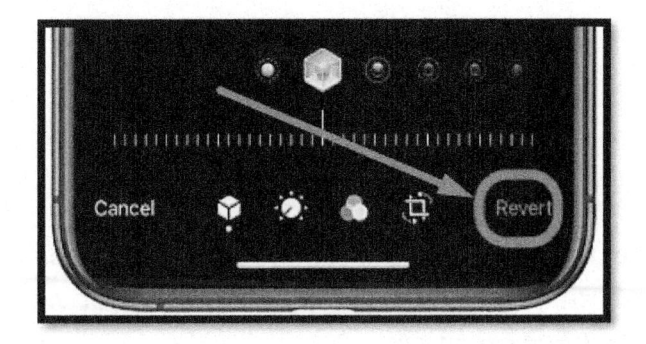

5. Tap **Revert to Original** to return your picture to its original state.

6. While you can't erase modifications after you've returned to the original shot, you can always re-edit it if you change your mind.

Frequently Asked Questions

1. How do you navigate through the Photos app?
2. How do you share and delete photos?
3. How do you import and export videos?
4. What are the different methods of sending long recorded videos on your iPhone?
5. How do you add text to your images?
6. How do you recover deleted images?
7. How do you hide and access your images?
8. How do you adjust your screen brightness?

CHAPTER SIX
FACETIME

Overview

FaceTime is a video and audio calling application available to Apple users and with your iPhone 15 Series; you can reach a Mac user via either audio or video. Chapter six talks about FaceTime and how you can use it.

How to set up FaceTime

Check that your iPhone 15 Series is running the most current iOS version (iOS 17). Use the following processes to check for updates and install them if necessary:

- Launch the "**Settings**" app on your iPhone.
- Swipe down and choose "**General**."
- Next, choose "**Software Update**." If a new version is available, select "**Download and Install**." To complete the update, follow the directions on the screen.

Log in with your Apple ID

FaceTime requires you to be signed in with your Apple ID. If you haven't already signed in, do the following:

- To begin, open the "**Settings**" app.
- Scroll down and choose "**FaceTime**."
- Click "**Sign In**" and enter your password and Apple ID. If you don't have an Apple ID or forgot it, you can create one by clicking "**Don't have an Apple ID or forgot it?**" and following the on-screen instructions.

Turn on FaceTime

After connecting with your Apple ID, FaceTime must be enabled:

- Check the "**FaceTime**" toggle in the "**FaceTime**" section of your iPhone's settings. If it is green, FaceTime is operational.
- Verify your email and phone number. Make sure your phone number and email address are correctly confirmed so that people can contact you over FaceTime.

- Navigate to the "**FaceTime**" settings page and choose "**You can be reached by FaceTime at**."
- Confirm that your email address and phone number are listed. If not, click to choose or add them.
- Enable Caller ID by entering the phone number or email address you wish to use as your FaceTime Caller ID.
- Navigate to the "**FaceTime**" settings and choose "**Caller ID**."
- Select a phone number or email address.
- FaceTime contacts can be added. To make a FaceTime call, you must have the other person's contact information in your iPhone address book.
- Open the "**Phone**" app, then the "**Contacts**" app.
- Select an existing contact or create a new one.
- Check to see whether the contact has a FaceTime phone number or email address.

Open FaceTime

You are now ready to begin a FaceTime call:

- Choose a contact by using the "**FaceTime**" app, or by using the "**Contacts**" or "**Phone**" applications.
- Tap the **FaceTime video camera icon** that appears next to the contact's name.
- You can start a FaceTime call while on a regular phone call by tapping the FaceTime sign.
- You can further customize your FaceTime experience by adjusting options such as camera effects, audio and video quality, and others:
- Go through the options under "**FaceTime**" and tweak them to your liking.

How to make and receive a FaceTime call

Make a FaceTime Call

Follow these steps to make a FaceTime video call:

- Launch the **FaceTime app**.
- To begin a new call, tap the **plus button** in the upper right corner.
- In the search box, enter the contact's name, phone number, or email address.
- Choose a contact from the list.
- Select **Video** to begin the video call.

Receive a FaceTime Call

Follow these procedures to receive a FaceTime video call:

- When you get a FaceTime call, the name and picture of the caller will be shown on your iPhone 15 Series.
- To accept the call, swipe the **green Answer button**.
- Your video stream will be shown, and you will be connected.

Record a video message

If no one answers your FaceTime video call, you can record a video message to express your message.

Here are the steps:

1. Wait for the countdown (from 5 to 1) before recording your message by tapping **Record Video**.

2. Tap ⬆ to send your recorded message, or **Retake** to rerecord it. You may also save it to Photos by tapping **Save**.
3. The receiver is alerted once you submit your video message.

Do not forget that you can only receive video messages from stored contacts, individuals you've contacted, and Siri-suggested persons.

Leave a voicemail

If the person you're calling doesn't answer your FaceTime audio call and you're a known contact of theirs (either in their contacts or you've messaged or talked to them lately), you'll be asked to leave a voicemail. If the person you're contacting has Live Voicemail enabled in **Settings > Phone**, your message will be transcribed on their screen as you speak, informing them of the reason you're calling and offering them the option to pick up the phone. Note that Live Voicemail is only accessible in English in the United States and Canada, except in Guam, Puerto Rico, and the United States. The British Virgin Islands.

Call again

To make another FaceTime call, perform one of the following:

- On the Record Video screen, tap **Call Again**.
- Tap the name or number of the person (or group) you want to call again in your call history.

During a FaceTime call

You can do the following during a FaceTime call:

- **Change Cameras**: Tap the camera icon to switch between your front and rear cameras.
- **Mute Audio**: Tap the microphone symbol to mute or unmute your audio.
- **Stop the Call**: Tap the red phone sign to stop the call.

How to use Memoji on FaceTime

This is how Memoji works with FaceTime:

Create a Memoji: If you haven't already, you must first make a Memoji.

Here's how to create one:

- Open the "**Messages**" app on your iPhone.
- Start a new conversation or join an existing one.
- Next to the text box, press and hold the **Animoji icon**, which looks like a monkey's face?
- Swipe to the right and choose "**New Memoji**."
- Change the appearance of your Memoji by picking various features such as eyes, nose, mouth, skin tone, and hairstyle.
- When you're satisfied with the appearance of your Memoji, press the "**Done**" button.
- Open the FaceTime app on your iPhone. The logo is green and has a white video camera.
- To start a new FaceTime call, tap the "**+**" button in the top right corner and enter a contact's name or phone number. You can also participate in an ongoing FaceTime conversation.

You can use your Memoji in a variety of ways during a FaceTime session.

- While on a call, slide up from the bottom of the screen to view the call controls to switch to Memoji. The Memoji symbol should be displayed (a smiling face with a star). Select this symbol.
- **Choosing Your Memoji**: If you have more than one Memoji, swipe left or right to choose one.
- **Memoji and Animoji Effects**: Use a variety of effects throughout the call. These effects will use your iPhone's TrueDepth camera to detect your facial expressions. Memoji will mimic your facial emotions such as smiling, frowning, or lifting your brows.
- **Stickers and Filters**: You can further personalize your Memoji by adding stickers and filters. Simply tap the **star icon** to get access to them.
- As you use your Memoji, drag it across the screen. You can also use pinch-to-zoom gestures to change the size and direction of the Memoji. Simply slide your Memoji off the screen to remove it.
- Swipe down after using your Memoji for the length of the call to return to the conventional FaceTime controls or to exit the Memoji interface.

How to start a FaceTime Audio/Video call from messages

To make a FaceTime Audio or Video call from your iPhone 15 Series' Messages app, follow these steps:

- To begin, unlock your iPhone using Face ID or your password.
- Navigate to your home screen and choose the Messages app. It is represented by a green speaking bubble icon.
- Choose an existing discussion/conversation with the person you want to call or press the compose icon (typically a pencil or paper icon) in the top-right corner to start a new one.
- To choose a contact, tap their name or picture at the top of the screen during the conversation. This will disclose their phone number.
- On the contact information page, you have various options, including buttons for both voice and video chats.
- To begin a FaceTime video call, tap the **video camera icon**.
- To begin a FaceTime Audio call, tap the **phone icon**.
- The call will connect if the other person is available and has FaceTime. You will either see their video or hear their voice, depending on whether you began a video or audio call.
- To end the call, use the "**End Call**" button or the red phone icon. As a consequence, the call will be terminated.

Remember that for FaceTime calls to work, both you and the person you're seeking to contact must have FaceTime enabled and be connected to the internet via Wi-Fi or cellular connection.

How to create a link to a FaceTime call

Create a link to a FaceTime call and send it to a friend or a group (via Mail or Messages) on FaceTime. They may join or start a call by clicking on the link. **Here are the steps:**

1. Launch the **FaceTime app**, and then tap the **Create Link button** at the top of the screen.
2. Select a method for distributing the link (email, messages, etc.).

You can plan a remote video conference in Calendar by providing a FaceTime connection as the meeting location. Ask anybody to join you in a FaceTime call, even those who do not own an Apple device. They may participate in one-on-one and group FaceTime calls from their browser—no login required. (They must use the most recent version of Chrome or Edge, and sending video needs H.264 video encoding capabilities.)

How to turn on live captions for FaceTime calls

You can generally enable live captioning for FaceTime calls on the iPhone 15 Series using the accessibility settings. **The steps are as follows:**

- Locate and open the "**Settings**" app on your iPhone.
- Scroll down to find the "**Accessibility**" option in the Settings menu; it frequently contains an icon of a wheelchair-user.
- An "**Audio/Visual**" or analogous option should be included in the "Accessibility" menu. Then tap on the option.
- There is an option for "**Live Captions**" or "**Transcripts**" in this section. This is the location where the feature would be enabled.
- Hit this button to initiate FaceTime calls with live captioning. Depending on how the implementation is done, you can also have additional customization options for the captions, such as font style and size.
- After closing the "**Accessibility**" settings, return to your home screen. Call someone on FaceTime or use the FaceTime app.
- During a FaceTime call, the other person's statements should be translated in real time using live subtitles that show on the screen.

How to include background sounds on a FaceTime call

Here are the steps:

- Make sure your iPhone is running the most current version of iOS. Install any available updates by going to "**Settings**" > "**General**" > "**Software Update**".
- Launch the FaceTime app on your iPhone.
- Select the person you want to chat with from your contacts list or enter their contact information to begin a FaceTime session.
- You may be able to enable background sounds while on a FaceTime call if it is available. This feature is accessible when on a call via the call settings or a separate menu.

- If the feature is enabled, you should be able to pick a background sound for your FaceTime call from a list. This might include options such as rain, ocean waves, or other background sounds.
- You can adjust the volume of the background sound to your liking.
- After picking your background music and setting the volume, continue with the FaceTime call as usual.

How to share your screen on a FaceTime call

To share your screen during a FaceTime chat, follow the instructions below:

- First of all, make sure your iPhone is running the most current version of iOS. Go to **"Settings" > "General" > "Software Update"** and follow the steps to update your iPhone.
- Open the **FaceTime app** on your iPhone and initiate a call with the person with whom you wish to share your screen.
- When on a FaceTime call, look for the in-call options. These options are usually found near the bottom of the screen.
- You should be able to share your screen if your iPhone supports it. This might be represented with an icon that looks like a monitor or screen.
- To share your screen, press the button. You may be prompted to share your whole screen, certain programs, or information.
- Depending on the settings available, you can share your whole screen, a specific application, or content such as a photo or document. Follow the on-screen instructions to make your selection.
- Once you've determined what to share, double-check your choice. Your screen will now be visible to the person on the other end of the FaceTime connection.
- You can end a screen-sharing session at any time by using the stop-sharing button. This button is normally positioned in the same location as when you began a screen-sharing session.

How to blur the background using portrait mode

You can blur the background during a FaceTime conversation by doing the following:

- Check to see whether your iPhone supports FaceTime Portrait Mode. Some iPhones enable background blur in portrait mode; validate that your device supports this feature.

- Open the FaceTime app. It is usually a white video camera with a green sign.
- To start a FaceTime call, choose an existing contact or add a new one by pressing the + sign.
- During the call, look for the "**Portrait**" or "**Background Blur**" options. It's usually a slider or a button with an aperture or a human symbol on it. To enable Portrait mode, tap this symbol.
- Typically, a slider is used to adjust the amount of blur in the background. With a slide, you may change the blur level. This allows you to keep your face concentration as the background blurs.
- Check the preview to ensure the background is properly blurred. If you're okay with the blur level, continue with the FaceTime conversation as usual.

Take a Live Photo in FaceTime on an iPhone

Snap a FaceTime Live Photo while on a video chat in the FaceTime app to record a moment of your discussion (not available in all countries or regions). The camera records everything that occurs shortly before and after you snap the shot, including the audio, so you can see and hear it exactly as it occurred later. **To take a FaceTime Live Photo, go to Settings > FaceTime and switch on FaceTime Live Photos, then perform one of the following:**

- If you're on the phone with someone else, tap ◯.
- During a Group FaceTime session, touch the tile of the person you wish to picture, then tap ⤢ and ◯.

You are both notified that the picture has been shot, and the live picture is stored in your Photos app.

Frequently Asked Questions

1. How do you set up FaceTime?
2. How do you make and receive a FaceTime call?
3. How do you record a video message and leave a voicemail on FaceTime?
4. How do you use Memoji on FaceTime?
5. How do you create a link to a FaceTime call?
6. How do you turn on live captions for FaceTime calls?
7. How do you share your screen on a FaceTime call?

CHAPTER SEVEN
MEMORY MOVIES

Overview

Chapter seven talks about creating and using memory movies including changing the memory mix on your iPhone 15 Series.

How to create a memory movie

For the vast majority of us, our iPhones are the only cameras we need and possess. At any one time, our phones are inundated with photographs. No, not only photographs but also memories. We don't only build memories in our lives now; we also capture them. And, thanks to the Memories function in Photos, our iPhones can turn those memories into a perfect montage suitable for them.

What exactly are iPhone Memories?

After detecting notable people, locations, and events in your library, the iPhone curates memories on your iPhones. After adding photographic effects and related tunes to the memory, it then shows them in a montage.

These memories may be seen and shared with friends and family. You can also use the memory slideshow on your Home screen's Photos widget. The iPhone selects photographs, music, and memories on its own, but you can modify anything. You may also make your memories.

When you make a memory, the only thing you have to do is choose the photographs or videos you want to include (if you're working from an album). You do not need to complete the remaining difficult tasks. The montage will be created automatically by the Photos app.

Editing Pre-Made iPhone Memories

On your iPhone, launch the **Photos app**. From the bottom of the screen, choose the **'For You'** tab.

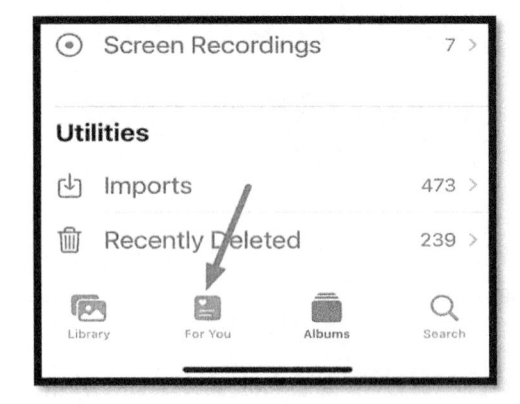

- In the upper part, you'll see the Memories that the iPhone has selected for you. Tap **'See All'** to access all of your iPhone's memories.

- To play a Memory, tap it.
- Tap the memory again to bring up the options. On the screen, a few alternatives would display.
- The photos or movies in the memory may be seen at the bottom. To see all of the photos or movies in the memory, tap **'Browse'** in the bottom right corner.

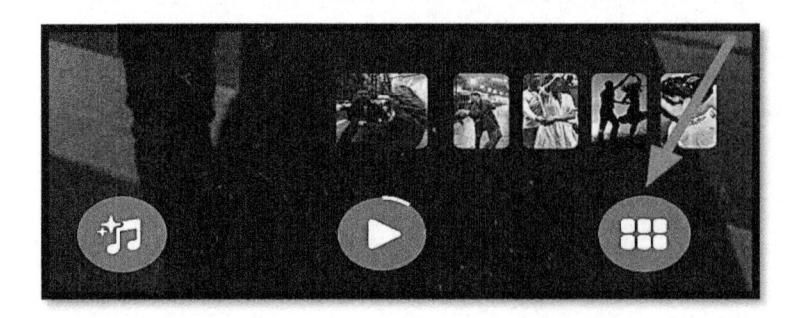

- When you hit Browse, the memory will continue to play if you haven't already stopped it, allowing you to browse through all of the photos.
- Holding and tapping a picture brings up choices like erasing it from memory, deleting it entirely from the library, and making it the key photo, among others. Simply tapping a picture will take you back to that photo in the memory slideshow.

How to share your favorite memories

The steps:

1. After creating the video, select **Done > Share Icon > Save Video**, and the memories video will be downloaded to your iPhone.
2. It will take some time to download the video. Tap the share symbol again after the download is complete to share it with others.

How to change the memory mix

- Tap the **'Memory mix'** icon on the bottom left to change the memory mix, i.e., the music or the photographic appearance.

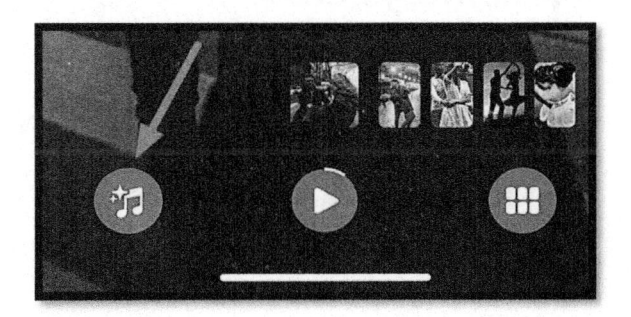

- In addition to the current song and photographic appearance (i.e., filter), the iPhone will show a few additional song and photographic style choices. Swipe across them to get a preview. At the bottom, you can see the song's title and the filter. Simply touch the memory frame to pick one, and you'll be returned to the slideshow page with new options.
- Aside from the curated combinations offered by the iPhone, users can also modify the memory appearance (filter), and those running iOS 17 can change the soundtrack. If you have an Apple Music subscription, you can choose any song from your collection, songs recommended to you based on your preferences, music played at the time the memory was created, or search the complete Apple Music catalog accessible in your location.
- To modify the appearance of the memory, hit the **'Filters'** button in the bottom right corner.

- Tap **'Done'** after selecting the new filter.

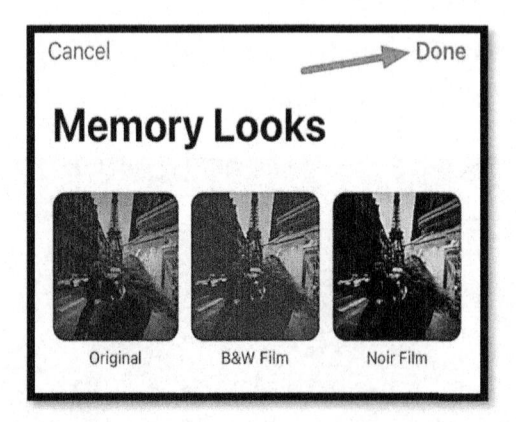

- Tap the **'Music'** button to change the memory music.

- Choose a song from the options on your screen or do a music search. Tap the song to pick it, and it will begin playing. If you don't want to, touch **'Cancel'** and choose another music. Otherwise, tap the **'Done'** button.

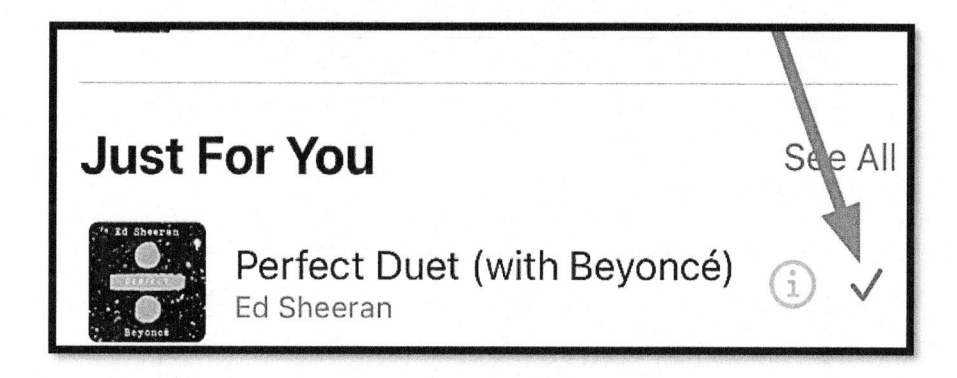

Manually Creating a Memory on Your iPhone

While learning how to alter pre-made memories is difficult enough, learning how to generate them from the start is far more difficult. Many people are unaware that such an option is available to them. However, once you understand the technique, the whole procedure becomes pretty simple.

You can select to create a memory from various locations. You may make a memory out of:

- An album
- A day or month from the library's calendar. The Year's images do not have this option.
- The People's Album

Creating a Memory from an Album or Day/ Month

The method for making a memory from an album, a day, or a month is the same. If the images do not belong in a certain album or day/month area, just create a new album with them.

1. Navigate to the library's album or day/month and press the **'More'** icon (three-dot menu) in the top-right corner.

2. Tap the **'Play Memory Movie'** option from the menu.

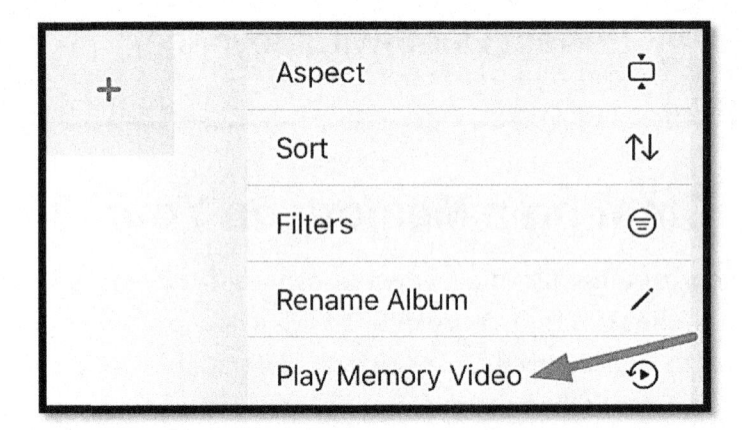

3. By selecting a music and photographic style on its own, the iPhone will generate a memory slideshow for the images in the album or the day/month. You can adjust the memory mix in the same way as you can edit pre-made memories. There will be a few handpicked song and filter combinations from which to choose. Alternatively, you can choose everything from the music and filter it yourself.

4. Tap the screen to bring up options if you want to store the memory. Then, in the top-right corner of the screen, hit the **'More'** option (three-dot menu). From the menu, choose **'Add to Favorites'**. The recollection will show in the **'For You'** tab's Memories section.

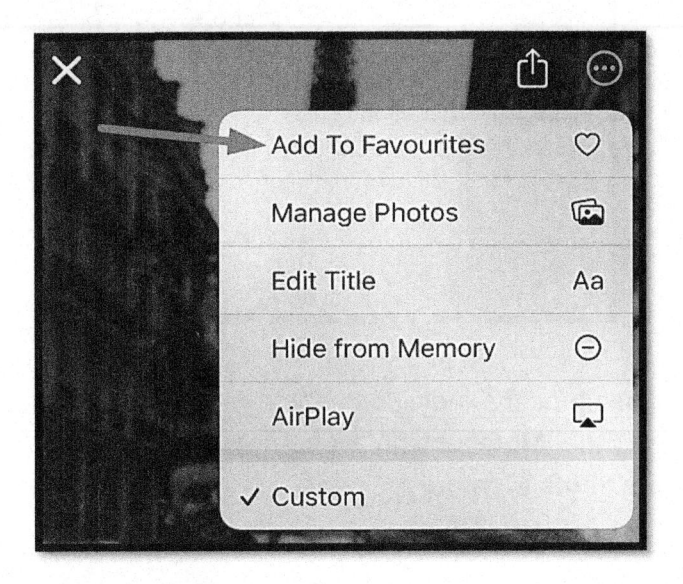

5. To close the memory, use the **'Close'** (X) button.

Creating a Memory for a Person

6. Go to the **'Albums'** menu to make a memory for someone.

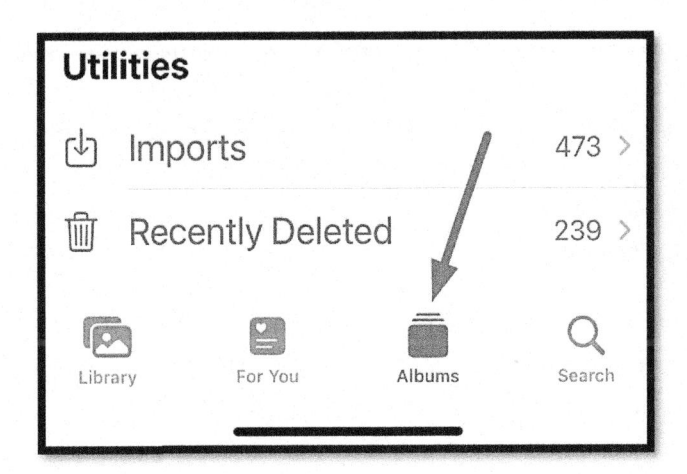

7. Move to the **'People'** album.

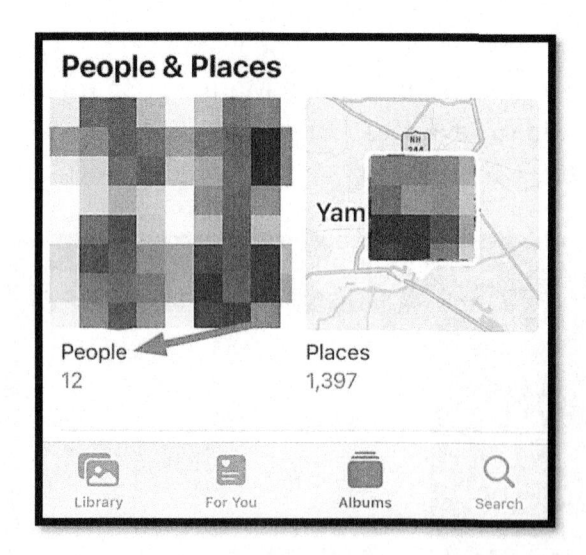

8. Tap the thumbnail for the individual. Their images will be shown. In the upper-right corner, tap the **'More'** button (three-dot menu).
9. Tap the **'Create Photo Memory'** button.

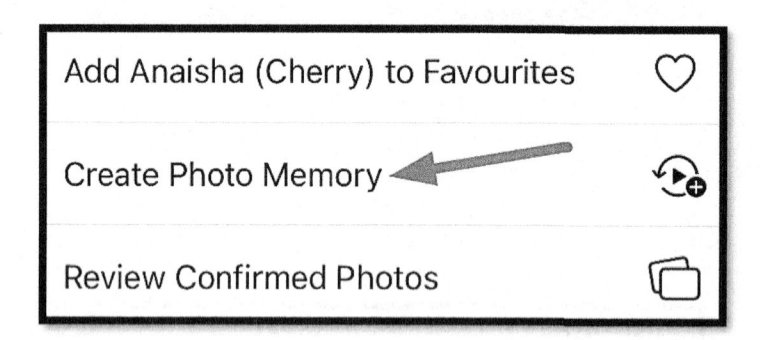

10. The memory slideshow will be displayed in the **'For You'** tab's Memories section. You can see it there. You can modify it exactly like any other iPhone memory.

Editing a Memory

You can change specific features of a memory, whether it's a pre-made memory or one you produced. You can also change its name, length, and add or delete photographs. Naturally, the possibilities differ based on the kind of memory.

Changing the Title

IPhone names your memories at random, sometimes based on location, day, album, person's name, or any context it detects, such as "**Celebration**." However, you can modify the name. To change the name of a memory, open it and press it to bring up options. In the upper-right corner, tap the **'More'** button (three-dot menu).

11. Choose **'Edit Title'** from the drop-down menu.

12. Change the name and then hit the **'Save'** button.

How to add and remove photos within memory

Here are the steps:

13. Tap **'More'** and then **'Manage images'** from the menu to add or delete images.

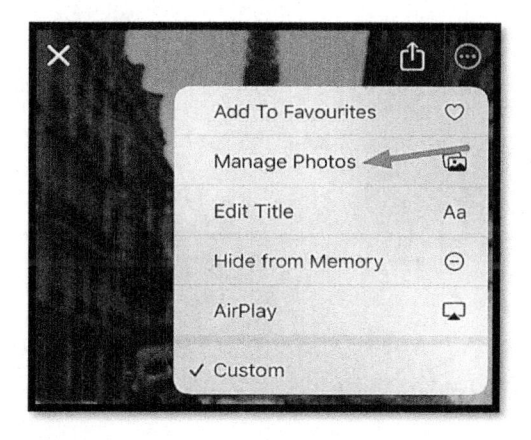

127

14. Select or deselect the photos to be added or deleted. Tap the **'Done'** button.

15. Pause the memory on the photo to make another photo the key photo instead of the current one. Tap **'More'** and then choose **'Make Key Photo'** from the menu.

Adjust the Length

Change the duration of pre-made memories. The option is not accessible for the memories you create since their length is "**Custom**". Tap **'More'** to access the iPhone's memories. There will most likely be three options: **'Short,' 'Medium,' and 'Long'.** Tap the desired selection. Depending on the number of photographs you have, you can only see **'Short'** and **'Medium'** for certain memories.

IPhone Memories are a terrific way to remember some of the best occasions in your life. You can also quickly distribute them to friends and relatives.

Protect the Memories Video

After learning "how to create memories slideshow on iPhone," you will have some films capturing treasured times or holidays that you may want to view often, but video loss may occur due to limited storage space, a change of mobile phone, or other factors.

Backup iPhone Memory Videos Using iCloud

In general, if you activate iCloud backup on your iPhone, iCloud will back up all of your iPhone's data and movies. As a result, you can use iCloud Photos on your iPhone to backup memory movies. **Here are the steps:**

16. Navigate to **Settings > Select iCloud** from your profile.

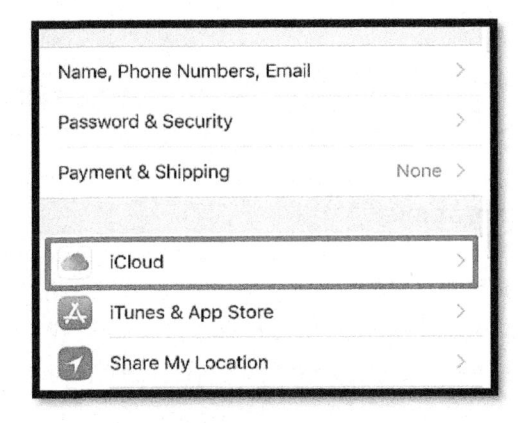

17. Select photos, and then turn on iCloud Photos to back up your photos and videos to the cloud.

iCloud photos will automatically backup all photos and videos on your iPhone, not only movies. Since iCloud automatically backs up your data, if you don't remove useless photos and movies on time, your iCloud will become a mess.

How to create new albums in the Photos app

Most of us have dealt with the issue of an overflowing picture collection at some time in our lives. The images app displays a jumble of screenshots, images of people, events, and aesthetic graphics, all of which you probably don't want to let go of. Fortunately, the Photos app's categories and albums will help you to arrange all of your photos so you can always locate what you're searching for without having to erase anything.

What Is the Difference Between an iPhone Folder and a Photo Album?

The distinction is obvious. You can simply upload images of a person, occasion, or event to an album to group them. A folder, on the other hand, allows you to add existing albums and other folders to it rather than individual photographs. Use this to group images of your holidays together, for example.

You may make an album with all of your images from your trip to Germany and another album with photos from your holiday to Spain. You can then create a folder called "**Vacations**" and add these two albums to it to keep them together. You may keep adding albums as you travel the globe! Isn't it amazing? You may even divide particular excursions into subfolders and create other albums inside them for specific events, locations, and happenings on your trip.

How to Create an Album in Photos

On an iPhone, you can easily organize images of a person or event by creating an album in the images app.

Here's how to put together an album:

1. Launch the **Photos app** and go to the **Albums menu**.
2. Click the plus (+) sign in the upper-left corner.
3. From the dropdown menu, choose **New Album**.

4. Type in the album's title and click **Save**.

5. Select all of the photos you want to include in your album and click **Add**. You can choose from All Photos or already created Albums.

If you want to add additional images to your album, just scroll down to the bottom of the album. A photo icon with a plus (+) sign will appear next to your most recent image. Tap it to start uploading new photos. When you're finished, hit **Add** in the bottom right corner, and all of your photos will be uploaded. Alternatively, open the album to which you want to add images and choose the symbol with three horizontal dots to Add images, Rename the Album, Delete the Album, Share Photos, and other options.

How to Create a Folder in Photos

Creating a folder allows you to collect many albums in one location. This is beneficial in a variety of ways and enables you to simply de-clutter your camera roll.

Let's see how you can create a folder in the Photos app:

1. Launch the **Photos app** and go to **Albums**.
2. Tap the **plus (+) sign** in the upper-left corner.
3. Select **New Folder**.

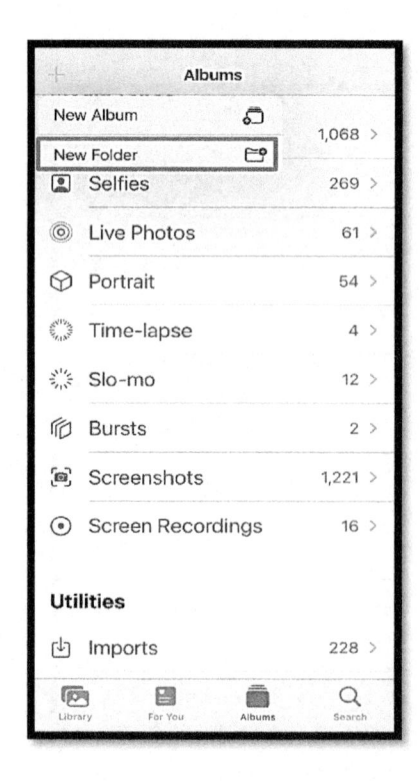

4. Enter a name for your folder and click **Save**. Your folder has now been created.

How to Add an Album to a Folder

You must first create an album before you can add it to a folder. Creating a new album inside your new folder follows almost the same basic processes, except you must first open the folder.

Here's what you should do:

1. Navigate to the folder to which you want to add a new album or folder.
2. Click the **Edit button** in the upper-right corner.
3. Tap the addition (+) symbol. Choose a **New Album or New Folder** based on your preferences.

4. Enter a name, click **Save**, and you're done. You can add photos to your new album.

How to Move an Existing Album into a Folder on iPhone

Assume you already have an album in your Photos app that you wish to transfer to your new folder. So, what do you do now? **While there is no simple way to do this, here is an easy and basic method:**

1. As instructed previously, create a New Album in your folder.
2. A popup box will appear, allowing you to pick the images you want to add to the album in your folder. Select Album from the bottom icons and tap on the album you wish to transfer to your new folder.
3. Select all of the photos in the album and hit the Add button.
4. Tap **Done**.
5. You should now remove the original album to prevent having a duplicate.

Even when using the iOS drag-and-drop approach, selecting all of the photos in your album may be tough. **In such a scenario, you have an even simpler option:**

18. In your folder, create a **New Album**. Instead of dragging and dropping all of your photos, just choose one and hit **Add**.
19. Navigate to the album you want to transfer to the new folder.
20. Tap **Select** in the upper-right corner, then **Select All** in the upper-left corner. With a single touch, this will automatically pick all of the photos in the album.
21. Click the three horizontal dots symbol in the bottom-right corner.
22. Tap **Add to Album**. Tap on your folder, then the album in the folder where you want it to go.

23. After that, remove the previous album to keep the Photos app tidy and organized.

Folders and albums are excellent for establishing a well-organized picture gallery. Albums let you upload photographs to classify and organize them together, while folders let you save several albums in one location. You can experiment with albums and folders to keep your images arranged the way you want.

How to Change a Photo Album's Cover Photo

Sorting your iPhone's photo library into albums helps browsing through them simpler and saves you time reading through the innumerable photographs you've shot over the years. To make your picture albums even more helpful, you can change the cover photo of each album so you can see what photos are in it at a glance.

How to Change the Cover Photo of an Album in Photos

When you create a photo album on your iPhone, the first photo in that album is used as the cover photo by default. The first picture in an album isn't always the ideal choice for the cover shot, which is why Apple makes it so simple to modify.

Simply follow these instructions to get started:

24. Launch the **Photos app** and go to **Albums**.
25. Choose the album whose cover image you want to modify.
26. Select the picture you want to use as the new cover photo.
27. Hold the picture down until a popup menu displays. Choose **Make Key Photo**.

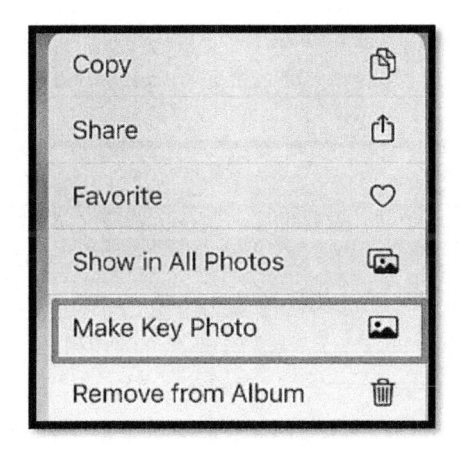

28. The selected picture will now replace the album's previous cover image.

How to Delete Unnecessary Photo Albums

When you download certain applications, such as Facebook or Snapchat, they will automatically generate picture albums. Having too many albums might cause your picture collection to become disorganized, depreciating photo albums in general. Many people are unaware that they may remove these picture albums from their iPhones. You can erase all iPhone picture albums except Recents and Favorites.

Here are the steps:

29. Navigate to the **Albums page** in the Photos app. Tap the Albums icon in the lower section to move to the My Albums page.

30. When you're on the Albums page, tap **See All** in the upper-right corner. This will provide a list of all your albums and the number of photos in each.
31. There is an **Edit button** in the upper right-hand corner. Tap this, and an option to create new albums and folders will appear in the top-left corner. Albums may now be rearranged to modify their order.
32. Every album that you can remove will also have red circles around it.

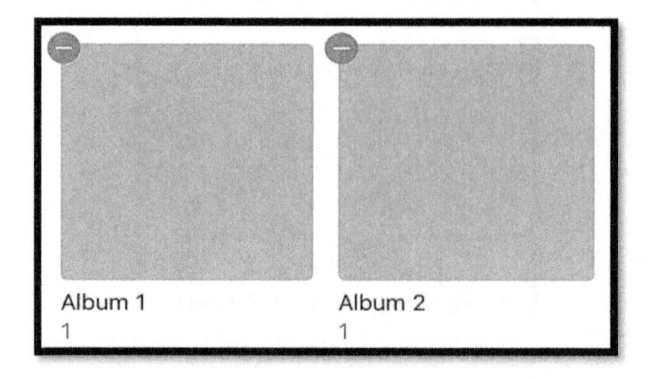

136

33. Tap the red circle to remove these albums. You will get an alert advising you that deleting the album will not destroy the images. Tap **Delete Album** and the album will be deleted. These photos will still be accessible via your Recents folder or the Library page.

How to Organize Photos in an Album

The steps:

1. On your iPhone, launch the **Photos app**.
2. The app should open to the "**Photos**" page by default, which shows all of your images and videos in chronological order.
3. **To arrange your photos, choose the ones you want to work with. You can do this in numerous ways:**
- Select specific photos by tapping on them.
- To choose several photos, hit the "**Select**" button in the upper right corner, then tap on each one.
- To choose a group of photos, touch the first photo and then drag your finger across the screen.
4. **Create Albums**:
- To create a new album, touch the "**+**" icon in the upper left or lower right corner of the screen.
- Create a title for your album.
- Select photos to add to the new album by touching "**Add**."
5. **Arrange Albums**:
- Tap the "**Albums**" tab at the bottom of the screen to see your albums.
- You can reorganize your albums by tapping "**See All**" and then holding and dragging the albums.
6. **Delete or Edit Photos in an Album**:
- Navigate to the album you want to change.
- Tap the "**Select**" button in the upper-right corner.
- Select the photos you want to modify or remove by tapping on them.
- At the lower part of the screen, you can add, share, or remove photos.
7. **Upload Photos to an Album**:
- Navigate to the album to which you want to add images.
- Tap the "+" sign.
- Choose the photos you want to include, and then touch "**Done**."

8. **Use Smart Albums and Categories**: The photos app also has features like "**Memories**" and "**For You**" that automatically arrange photos into collections and recommend activities based on your photos.
9. **Search for Photos**: Use the photo search function to discover images based on individuals, locations, objects, or even text. Simply choose the "**Search**" option and type in your search term.

How to identify and remove identical-looking images

In the Duplicates album, the photos app detects duplicate photographs and videos in your photo collection. Duplicate photos and videos can be merged to save space and tidy up your collection. The Merge tool integrated into Apple's photographs app is the simplest way to remove duplicate photos. It's quite fast and simple. Simply open the Photos app, tap the **Albums button** at the bottom of the screen, then scroll down to the bottom, and you can see an album called **Duplicates** under the **Utilities** area. If you don't see a duplicate album, the Photos app hasn't found any photographs that are duplicates. It's worth noting that Apple is playing it cautious with this function, requiring perfect matches or photographs that are extremely similar. Open the **Duplicates album** if you see it to view groupings of similar photographs. Tap any thumbnail to enlarge it. Swipe up to view the date and time, location, and other details. Click the Merge button on the right to merge the data, such as captions that may be on one but not the other, and enable the Photos app to choose the greatest quality picture. Select photos manually for additional control over the process. Choose the **Select** button in the upper right corner, and then select the thumbnails of the photographs you want to merge, and then use the **Merge button** in the lower center. You cannot combine images from different groupings.

How to Delete Burst Photos

The iPhone's burst picture mode may shoot a large number of photographs in a short period. Many of the images may be practically similar, particularly if you employ burst mode on an inanimate item by mistake. Unfortunately, duplicates inside a burst will not be detected by the Photos app. Instead, you must clear it up manually.

- Launch the **Photos app**, then go to the Albums tab at the bottom, scroll down to **Media Types**, and then touch **Bursts**.

- Tap any picture burst thumbnail to enlarge it, and then tap the **Select button** to bring up a photo carousel that you can scroll through by dragging side to side. The Photos app will emphasize the finest photos, with a gray dot appearing at the bottom of the screen below the thumbnails.
- Tap on your favorites to choose them. After a checkmark appears in the bottom right corner, click the **Done button** in the top right. You'll be presented with three possibilities. Choose to **Cancel** if you change your mind and want to modify your options. If you want the full burst as separate shots, choose **Keep Everything**. To preserve just the images you've chosen, choose to preserve X Favorites, where X is the number of photos you've chosen.
- The photos app will convert the burst photos into ordinary photos and preserve them in your library, allowing you to edit and share each one separately. The whole burst will be put in the Recently Deleted album and will stay there for 30 days. If you need to free up space on your iPhone right away, you may remove anything in the **Recently Deleted album manually**.

Is it bad that I have so many duplicates?

Any phone can take images, but the newer iPhone models are especially quick. There is also a burst mode that may be accessed by pressing a button. Volume down takes a single shot, and volume up takes a fast burst of around 10 photos per second. This can be turned off in the Settings app. locate the **Camera section** and disable **Use Volume Up for Burst**.

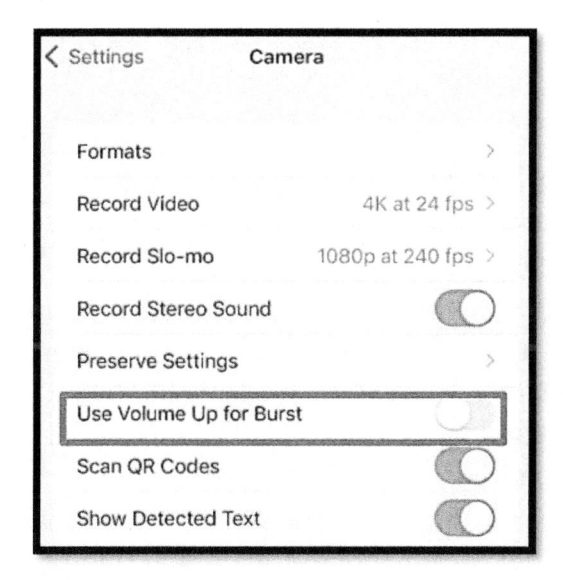

It's a fantastic thing to be able to snap full-resolution images quickly. Children's and animals pictures, which are famously rapid, may be out of focus or have motion blur. A burst is often required to freeze the action, but after 10 seconds you'll have 100 images, many of which are quite identical. When trying to get the ideal photo, it's a good idea to shoot thousands of shots with your iPhone. Outdoor illumination, in addition to micro-expressions, blinks, and fading grins, may alter significantly in seconds. With so many photos to pick from, you're more likely to locate some good portraits. Most photographers take images without thinking, which results in a few great shots and countless copies that are worthless or no longer required. Duplicate picture deletion or merging on your iPhone is an essential maintenance step that, like iOS system upgrades, should be done regularly. If you take a lot of images, checking for duplicates weekly can be a smart idea.

How to Rename Photos on iPhone

The naming convention for your screenshots is a confusing mess, regardless of whether you're using a Mac, iPad, iPhone, or even an Apple Watch. In actuality, there is a reason why screenshots are titled the way they are, but it's inconvenient if you want to look for anything.

How to quickly rename iPhone Screenshots

The only "**catch**" is that you can only name (or rename) screenshots on your iPhone when they are being recorded.

Here's how to go about it:

1. Go to the website or picture you want to screenshot.
2. Press the Side and Volume Up buttons simultaneously.
3. Quickly let go of both buttons.
4. When the snapshot preview shows in the bottom left corner, tap it.
5. Tap the **Share button** in the upper right corner of the Image Editor.
6. Tap **Rename** under the name of the snapshot.
7. Give the screenshot a name.
8. Click the **Submit button**.

You can then share the picture by scrolling down and clicking **Save to Files**, or by pressing the **X button** in the upper right corner of the Share Sheet. Then, in the upper left corner, press the **Done button**.

When asked, choose one of the following options:

- Save to Photos
- Save to Quick Notes
- Save to Files
- Delete Screenshot
- Cancel

Nothing will happen if you forget to rename the snapshot or accidentally swipe it away. However, the processes are a little more time-consuming.

Renaming Photos on iPhone

If you want to rename Photos on iPhone, it's a function that's been there for a while. However, the procedure is pretty lengthy, and we're still expecting that Apple would enable picture renaming directly from the Photos app. When it comes to adjusting images, there are already so many alternatives available that it's surprising that this hasn't been addressed yet.

Nonetheless, here's how you rename images on an iPhone:

1. On your iPhone, launch the **Photos app**.
2. Find the picture you want to rename.
3. Choose the picture.
4. Tap the **Share Sheet button** in the lower left corner.
5. Navigate and choose **Save to Files**.
6. Select the place where you want to save the screenshot.
7. Tap the picture title at the bottom of the page.
8. Give the picture a new name.
9. On your virtual keyboard, hit the **Done button**.

Change how photos appear in an album

You can change the size and aspect ratio of images in an album.

1. On your iPhone 15 Series, launch the **Photos app**.
2. Select **Albums**, and then select the album.
3. Then tap ⋯ , then choose one of the following options:

- Zoom Out

- Zoom In
- Aspect Ratio Grid

Frequently Asked Questions

1. How do you create a memory movie on your iPhone 15 Series?
2. How do you share your favorite memories?
3. How do you change the memory mix?
4. How do you create a memory from an album?
5. How do you add or remove photos within memory?
6. How do you protect the memories of a video?
7. How do you create a folder in photos?
8. How do you move an existing album into a folder?
9. How do you delete unnecessary photo albums?
10. How do you organize images in your album?

CHAPTER EIGHT
MACRO PHOTOGRAPHY AND OTHER CAMERA MODES

Overview

In this chapter, you will learn about macro photos, which devices support them, how to shoot macro photos, how to take pictures in portrait modes, and a host of others.

What exactly are Macro Photos?

Macro photography allows you to go up close to a subject and get extreme close-ups. A camera sensor must be capable of focusing on objects as close as 2-3 cm away. This technology has been introduced to the iPhone 15 Pro and iPhone 14 Pro lineups by Apple, enabling them to concentrate on objects as near as 2 cm away.

Which iPhones are capable of macro photography?

All iPhones that allow macro photography are listed below:

- iPhone 13 Pro
- iPhone 13 Pro Max
- iPhone 14 Pro
- iPhone 14 Pro Max
- iPhone 15 Pro
- iPhone 15 Pro Max

While the standard iPhone 13, iPhone 14, and iPhone 15 models have a 12MP ultra-wide shooter, capturing macro photographs on them is not natively feasible, which is one of the reasons why you should purchase a Pro iPhone model instead of the regular variations. There are, however, methods for taking macro photographs on an incompatible iPhone. When you are within 14cm of a subject, your iPhone will automatically convert to the macro camera. It is not feasible to disable this behavior.

How to Shoot Macro Photos on an iPhone 15 Series

To shoot macro photographs with your iPhone 15 Series, no extra app is required. The basic iPhone camera app is perfect enough.

1. Launch the Camera app. This is also applicable to the Pro Max versions.
2. Simply bring the phone near to the subject while in Photo mode. Make sure you're at least 14 cm away from it.
3. The ultra-wide camera on your iPhone will instantly convert to the macro lens and concentrate on the subject. The macro symbol in the lower-left corner of the viewfinder will indicate this.
4. To capture the picture, touch the shutter button. You can zoom close or use night mode to get macro images if necessary.
5. If you don't want to use the macro camera, turn it off on the left. You can also disable the Macro Control option in the iPhone 15 Pro's camera viewfinder by navigating to **Settings > Camera**.
6. In addition to macro images, the iPhone 15 series can shoot macro films. Swipe to the footage menu, approach the subject, turn on the macro camera, and begin capturing footage. You can also use the macro capability of the ultra-wide camera in slow-motion and time-lapse movie modes. Make sure there's enough light around while capturing macro images or movies for the best results. Otherwise, the image or video will be noisy.

How to use automatic macro switching control

You can choose when the camera changes to the Ultra-Wide camera to capture macro images and movies. **Here are the steps:**

1. Open the Camera app on your iPhone, and then approach the subject. ✿ displays on the screen when you are within macro distance of your subject.
2. Tap ✿ to disable automatic macro switching. Back up or tap 5x to swap to the Ultra-Wide camera if the picture or video gets hazy.
3. Tap ✿ to reactivate automatic macro swapping.
4. Go to **Settings > Camera**, then turn off **Macro Control** to disable automatic switching to the Ultra-Wide camera for macro photos and movies.
5. To save your Macro Control settings across camera sessions, go to **Settings > Camera > Preserve Settings**, then enable **Macro Control**.

How to shoot macro video in time-lapse or slow-motion

Here are the steps:

1. Open the **Camera app** on your iPhone and choose **Slo-mo or Time-lapse mode**.

2. Switch to the Ultra-Wide camera by tapping.5x, and then go closer to the subject.
3. To begin and stop recording, use the **Record button**.

How to take a picture in portrait mode

Apple's Portrait Mode has become a popular technique for iPhone users to take spectacular images with a depth-of-field effect known as bokeh, enabling them to capture a photo that keeps the subject crisp while blurring the backdrop. With the release of the iPhone 15, Apple has enhanced its portrait game even more, due to an updated camera system that allows for more detailed portraits and better low-light performance. Furthermore, iPhone 15 users can now capture portraits without ever switching to Portrait mode.

This is how it's done.

1. Aim the camera toward a human, dog, or cat while the Camera app is active.
2. Wait for a circle f symbol to appear in the viewfinder's bottom-left corner. If the symbol does not display, concentrate on a subject in the viewfinder.
3. Tap the f symbol to encircle it with a yellow circle.
4. When you're ready, press the shutter button to capture a portrait-style shot.

Your portrait image is now available to see by touching it in the Camera interface's upper right corner.

How to Turn Photos into Portraits after Shooting

When you snap a picture of a human, cat, or dog on iPhone 15, the camera identifies them in the frame and automatically records rich depth information, enabling you to transform it into a breathtaking portrait immediately or later in the Photos app.

This is how it's done:

Apple's Portrait Mode has become a popular technique for iPhone users to take spectacular images with a depth-of-field effect known as bokeh, enabling them to capture a photo that keeps the subject crisp while blurring the backdrop. Portrait photo mode on prior iPhones employed a more arduous approach than ordinary photos to record the depth map in the image, resulting in additional shutter latency and a lack of support for Smart HDR. However, on iPhone 15 models, Apple's new next-generation Portraits utilize the same Photonic engine pipeline as ordinary shots, so there are no quality or shutter latency compromises in any mode. That implies you may convert a photo of a person into a Portrait after the fact. When editing, it just takes a few touches.

Quickly Convert a Photo to a Portrait

The steps:

1. Tap any picture shot in picture mode to see it in full screen in the Photos app. If the picture has depth information, a Portrait button will show in the top-left corner.
2. To activate the depth of field effect, tap the **Portrait button** and pick **Portrait** from the dropdown menu.
3. If you don't like the effect, hit the **Portrait button again** and choose **Portrait Off** to turn it off.

Edit the Portrait Effect in Photos

Follow the steps below:

1. Tap any picture shot in picture mode to see it in full-screen in the Photos app. If the picture has depth information, a Portrait indication will be displayed in the top-left corner.
2. Select **Edit**.
3. In Photos, edit the Portrait Effect
4. Tap any picture shot in photo mode to see it in full-screen in the Photos app. If the picture has depth information, a Portrait indication will be displayed in the top-left corner.
5. Select **Edit**.
6. Proceed to edit the Portrait Effect in Photos.
7. Tap any photo shot in photo mode to see it in full-screen in the Photos app. If the picture has depth information, a Portrait indication will be displayed in the top-left corner.
8. Select Edit.
9. To reverse any portrait effects, just reopen the picture, choose **Edit**, and then **Revert**.

It's worth mentioning that the Live Photo effects aren't accessible when the portrait effect is applied to a Live Photo captured in Photo mode. Tap Live to see the Live Photo or to apply a Live Photo effect that does not include the portrait effect.

Turn off Auto Portrait Capture

Block the iPhone 15 camera from automatically recording depth information in images if you want to preserve storage space.

The steps:

1. Launch the **Settings app.**
2. Scroll down to **Camera**.

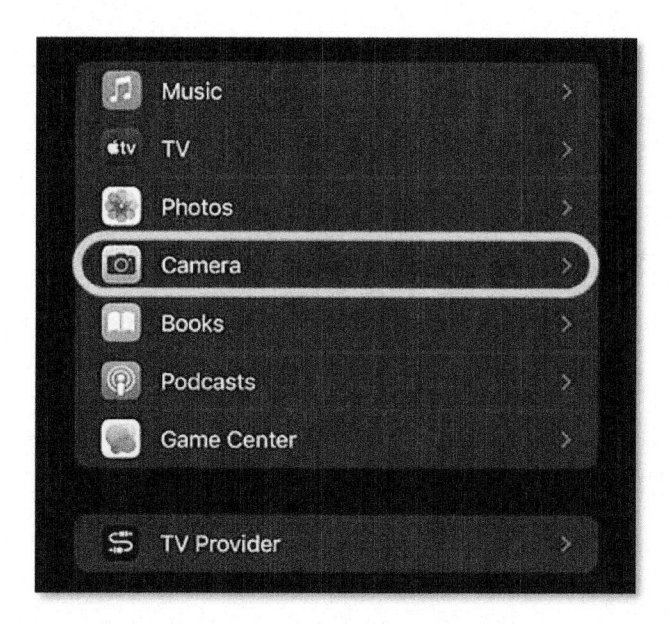

3. Move down and turn off the Portraits in Photo Mode option.

Adjust Depth Control and Portrait Lighting

After taking a picture in Portrait mode, you can change the amount of background blur and the strength of the Portrait Lighting effects.

Here are the steps:

1. Select a Portrait mode photo from your collection.
2. Tap **Edit**, and select the Depth Control or Portrait Lighting buttons at the top of the screen to alter Depth Control or Portrait Lighting. A slider is displayed underneath the image.

3. To change the effect, move the slider to the left or right. A gray dot above the slider represents the photo's original value.
4. Select **Done**.

Remove the Portrait mode effect

Follow the steps below:

1. Choose the picture you want to change.
2. Select **Edit**.
3. At the top of your screen, choose **Portrait**.
4. Select **Done**.

Return to **Edit** and select **Portrait again** if you change your mind and want to re-add the Portrait mode effect.

How to take a picture in night mode

Night mode revolutionized the way the iPhone shoots photographs in low-light situations. Night mode was introduced in 2019 and has since become a regular feature on other iPhone models.

How Does Night Mode Function?

In low-light circumstances, night mode helps you to capture more detail. It also brightens your shot, allowing you to see items that might otherwise be covered in the dark. It works for both outdoor and indoor images. You may take that humiliating snapshot of your sleeping pal and the starry sky. Night mode makes use of the bigger sensor that Apple has included in the iPhone 11 and subsequent iPhone models. This sensor allows for more light, allowing you to brighten a photograph in low-light conditions.

Night mode also makes use of the machine learning and Neural Engine capabilities built into Apple's A13 and subsequent mobile CPUs. When you select night mode, the camera detects the quantity of ambient light and determines how many frames it needs to take to generate a decent shot. The camera produces a series of images with varying exposure settings, some shorter than others. The iPhone then analyzes these photographs to produce a composite of the scene.

Which iPhones have night mode?

Unfortunately, night mode is not available on all iPhone models. It is also only accessible on certain lenses depending on the iPhone model. It is compatible with the iPhone 11 Series to the iPhone 15 Series.

How to Use Night Mode

The night mode is very simple to operate. Simply launch the camera app, and select **Photo**, and the iPhone will activate Night Mode in low-light circumstances. When the function is enabled, the Night mode symbol at the top of the screen becomes yellow. The time it takes to capture a night-mode shot is shown by the number next to the icon. You can toggle night mode on and off by tapping this symbol. Selecting Live or turning on the camera's flash will also deactivate night mode.

Change the capture time

When you snap a picture in Night mode, a number shows next to the Night mode symbol to indicate the duration of the photo. You can adjust the appearance of your picture by extending the capture duration.

- To access the camera settings, tap the arrow above the viewfinder.
- Select Night mode from the menu that displays below the viewfinder.
- Select **Max** from the slider above the shutter button to lengthen the capture duration.

When you snap the shot, the slider transforms into a timer that ticks down until the capture time expires.

Tips for Better Night Photography

Check below for the tips for better night shooting:

- **Use a tripod**: Keeping your camera motionless is essential while shooting in night mode. Any movement causes the image to blur. To keep your iPhone stable, use a tripod. If you don't have a tripod, brace your arms against your body or a substantial object, such as a table or your car's hood.
- **Not only for the dark**: Night mode can also be used in low-light situations. You can adjust the exposure duration to make the shot brighter or darker, giving it a

unique appearance. Play around with the settings to see what you can come up with.
- **Golden Hour**: Night mode is especially useful for dawn and sunset photographs, which often catch a variety of hues. To darken the shot, switch off night mode; to brighten the surroundings, turn it on. It's yet another tool for getting that ideal shot.

How to use live text with the camera

Live Text is a function on the iPhone that allows you to copy, paste, and share text directly from the Camera or Photos app. Text can be recognized by your iPhone in a handwritten letter, a business card, a nutrition label, a street sign, and a variety of other locations.

The benefit of Live Text?

- Using Live Text, save handwritten notes to other applications (such as the Notes app) so you can preserve or share the information without having to write it manually.
- Use iPhone Live Text to detect a restaurant sign, search it up, then share it with friends or book a reservation.
- You can translate and check text where you have your iPhone.

IPhone Photos: How to Use Live Text

Live Text for iPhone recognizes text in visual media using OCR (optical character recognition) technology, making it exceedingly easy to copy, paste, look up, share, and save text from the Photos and Camera apps.

Here's how to include Live Text onto photos using the iPhone Photos app:

- Launch the **Photos app**.
- Tap on the image with the text you want to select.
- Select the **Live Text icon**. When your iPhone Live Text function detects accessible text in a picture, this will show in the bottom-right corner.

A colorful box will appear around the identified text in Live Text.

1. Long press a word inside the highlighted area to choose part or all of the text.
2. Using the mouse or by tapping on individual words, choose the required text.

- You will see a toolbar with options like Copy, Select All, Look Up, Translate, and Share.
- To access additional choices, you need to press on the over arrow.
- To highlight all recognized text, tap **Select All**.

- Tap Look Up to learn more about the selected text.
- At the bottom of your screen, you'll notice a menu with definitions and other information for the text you picked using Live Text.
- Tap **Share** to share the selected text.
- You can send the text using Messages or another app, or choose another sharing option from the Share menu.
- Tap **Translate** to translate the text into another language. English, Spanish, French, Italian, Chinese, German, and Portuguese are now supported languages for Live Text.
- Use the Translate option at the bottom of the screen to translate the selected text and, if necessary, copy the translation. Swipe up to view the full Translate menu.

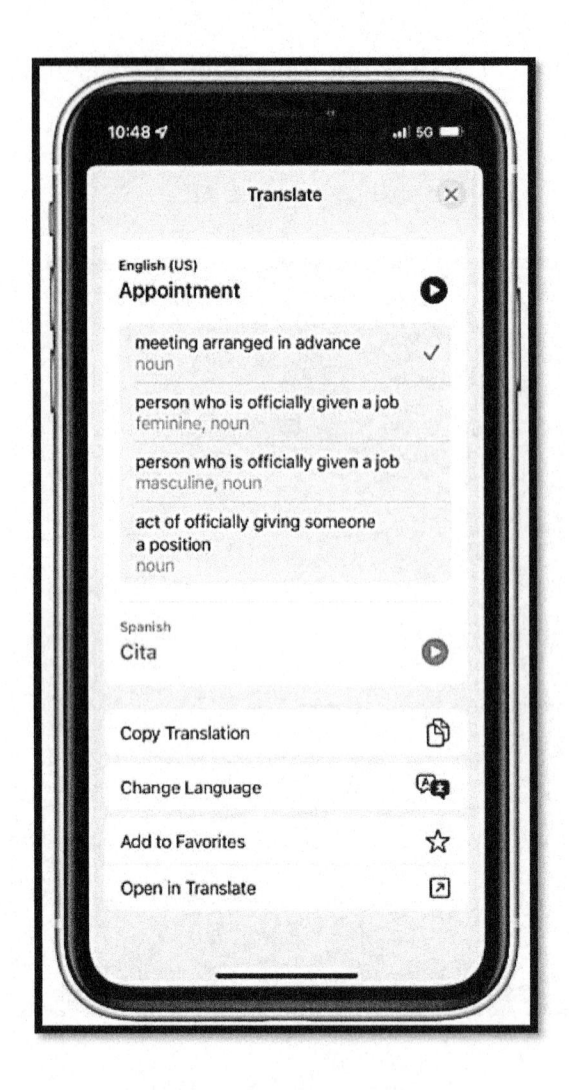

- Tap **Copy** to copy the chosen text and paste it into another app. You may copy and paste it into any other program, like Notes or Safari.

How to Use Live Text in the Camera on iPhone

Use Live Text to identify text before taking a photo. This enables you to utilize your iPhone as a live-lookup device for things like road signs, ads, and other time-sensitive text in the real world.

Here's how to use Live Text in the Camera app on your iPhone.

1. Launch the **Camera app**.
2. Point the camera at the text to be looked up, translated, shared, or copied.

3. In the lower-right corner of the screen, tap the **Live Text symbol.** This appears when your iPhone detects text in the camera's field of view.
4. Live Text will highlight text that has been identified.
5. If the camera only illuminates a portion of the text, you can always swipe or press a blank area of the screen, then tap another piece of text to concentrate Live Text on it.
6. After you've chosen the text, you'll see the same Copy, Select All, Look Up, Translate, and Share choices as in Photos with Live Text. To access additional choices, you may need to hit the over arrow.
7. At this point, you can use Live Text in the same manner as you would use it in a still photo. Your iPhone will store the text you're working on until you're finished.

How to use depth control

Follow these basic steps to use depth control in the iPhone camera app:

1. On your iPhone, open the Camera app by pressing the camera icon on the home screen.
2. When shooting in Portrait mode, depth control is often employed to produce a depth-of-field effect with a crisp subject and a blurred backdrop. Swipe the camera mode selection (typically placed above the shutter button) left or right until you see "Portrait."
3. After choosing Portrait mode, you can change the depth effect either before or after snapping a shot.

Before Taking a Photo

- Compose your photo such that your subject is in the frame.
- A slider with an f-number or "f-stop" sign should appear on the screen. The depth control is represented by this.
- To change the depth effect, slide your finger up or down on this control. Sliding up increases (lower f-number) background blur, whereas sliding down lowers (higher f-number).
- When you're happy with the effect, press the shutter button to capture the image.

After Taking a Photo

- After you've shot a picture in Portrait mode, you can change the depth effect.
- Launch the **Photos app** and choose the photo.

- Tap "**Edit**" in the upper right corner of the screen.
- A slider symbol representing depth control will appear. Tap it.
- Use the slider to adjust the depth effect, and then hit "Done" when you're satisfied with the outcome.

4. After capturing or editing a shot with depth control, you may save it to your Camera Roll.

How to upload your photos and keep them safe

Uploading and securing your images on an iPhone 15 series smartphone is critical to keeping your memories safe and accessible.

Here are the steps:

Use iCloud Photos

Apple's cloud storage service, iCloud images, is a wonderful method to keep your images secure and available across all of your Apple devices.

How to Enable iCloud Photos

- Open the "**Settings**" app on your iPhone.
- At the top, tap on your Apple ID.
- Select "**iCloud**" and then "**Photos**."
- Turn on "**iCloud Photos**."

Increase iPhone Storage

- If your iPhone's storage is running low, activate "**Optimize iPhone Storage**" in the "iCloud Photos" settings. This option saves full-resolution photos to iCloud while also storing reduced copies on your smartphone.

Backup to iCloud

Make sure your images are backed up to iCloud regularly.

Enable iCloud Backup

- Select "**Settings**."
- Enter your Apple ID.
- Tap "**iCloud**."

- Move to the bottom and choose "**iCloud Backup**."
- Turn on "**iCloud Backup**" and then tap "**Back Up Now**."

Use My Photo Stream

My Photo Stream automatically uploads and distributes your most recent photographs to iCloud across all of your Apple devices.

Enable My Photo Stream

- In "**Settings**," choose "**Photos**."
- Select "**My Photo Stream**."

Use AirDrop

Use AirDrop to swiftly send images from your iPhone to other Apple devices. It's a local, safe way to share images.

- To use AirDrop, launch the Control **Center** by swiping down from the upper-right corner of your screen.
- Hold down the Photos widget.
- Select the photos to share, then pick the recipient device and send them using AirDrop.

Save Photos to Files

Photos can be saved to the Files app and backed up to iCloud.

- Launch the **Photos app** and choose the image you want to save.
- Tap the **Share button** (an upward-pointing square).
- Select "**Save to Files**" and then an iCloud Drive destination.

Use third-party cloud services

Use third-party cloud storage services like Google Drive, Dropbox, or OneDrive as alternatives to iCloud. Download the applications, sign in, and then upload your photos.

Organize and delete unwanted photos regularly

Keeping your photo library clutter-free may help you conserve storage space and access your favorite photos more easily.

- Go through your images regularly and remove any duplicates or shots you no longer require.

Use Password Security and Biometrics

To safeguard your iPhone 15 Series, choose a strong password and use biometrics (Face ID). This helps to keep unauthorized people out of your images.

- Navigate to "**Settings**" and then "**Face ID & Passcode**."
- Turn on the passcode and Face ID.

Enable two-factor authentication

To add a degree of protection, enable two-factor authentication for your Apple ID.

- Navigate to "**Settings**" > "Your Name" > "Password & Security" > "Two-Factor Authentication."

Use a VPN for Additional Security

Consider using a VPN while sharing images over public Wi-Fi networks if you're worried about privacy and security.

Backup your photos locally

Back up your images to an external hard drive or your computer using iTunes or Finder regularly to offer an extra degree of protection.

How to scan QR codes

Scanning QR codes on the iPhone 15 series:

- Use Face ID or the power button to wake up your iPhone.
- Find the Camera app icon on your home screen and tap it to launch it.
- To scan a QR code, position your iPhone's camera such that the QR code is visible in the screen's viewfinder. Make sure the QR code is well-lit and in the middle of the frame.
- The camera should focus on the QR code automatically. If not, manually concentrate by tapping on the QR code on the screen.

- When the QR code is in focus and completely visible, your iPhone will identify it and show a notice banner at the top of the screen with the QR code's information. If it's a webpage, you can access it in Safari by tapping on the notice.
- Depending on the content of the QR code, you may be given many possibilities. If it's a website, for example, you can touch it to open it; if it's a contact card, you can add the contact to your address book; and if it's a Wi-Fi network, you may join it.
- View QR Code History

You can browse your QR code history to examine scanned QR codes:
1. Open the "**Settings**" app on your iPhone.
2. Scroll down and choose "**Camera**."
3. Select "**Scan QR Codes**" to see a history of codes scanned.

- (Optional) Enable QR Code Scanning from the Control Center:

If you routinely scan QR codes, you can save it to your Control Center for easy access.
- Open the "**Settings**" app on your iPhone.
- Move to the bottom and click "**Control Center**."
- Select "**Customize Controls**."
- Find "**QR Code Scanner**" and choose the green "**+**" symbol to add it to your Control Center.
- To use the QR code scanner, swipe down from the top-right corner of your screen and hit the QR code icon.

Here's how to run a QR code scanner from the Control Center:
- To access the Control Center, swipe down from the top-right corner of the screen.
- In the Control Center, look for the QR code scanner icon. It often takes the form of a little square containing a QR code. If it is not there, you may need to change the Control Center to incorporate a QR code reader.

If you don't see the QR code scanner icon, go to the iPhone's settings and add it. To do so:
- Open the "**Settings**" app.
- Swipe down and choose "**Control Center**."
- The option, "**QR Code Scanner**." should pop up when you select "**More Controls**." Tap the green plus sign (+) next to it to add it to your Control Center.
- To return to the Control Center from the Settings app, slide down (or up) from the screen's border.
- To use the QR code scanner, just hit the icon in the Control Center.

- After the iPhone's camera opens, you can scan a QR code by placing it inside the frame. Your iPhone 15 Series will automatically scan the QR code and alert you when it recognizes it. This might be the launch of an app, a website, or relevant information.

Frequently Asked Questions

1. How do you shoot macro photos and videos?
2. How do you use automatic macro switching control?
3. How do you shoot macro video in slow motion or in time-lapse?
4. How do you turn photos into portraits after shooting?
5. How do you adjust depth control and portrait lighting?
6. How do you capture an image in night mode?
7. How do you use Live Text in the camera app?
8. How do you scan QR codes?

CHAPTER NINE
TROUBLESHOOTING ISSUES

Overview

Your iPhone 15 series is expected to have one issue or the other as regards the camera. This chapter is dedicated to outlining the issues and possible solutions.

How to Solve Camera Crashes

It may be quite aggravating to have camera crashes or troubles with the camera app on your iPhone 15 series device.

Here are the steps:

Restart your iPhone

A quick restart may sometimes cure software problems that are causing the camera app to crash. Power off by pressing and holding the power button. Wait a few seconds before turning on your iPhone again.

Close Background Apps

Background applications may interfere with the functioning of the camera app. To use the App Switcher, swipe up from the bottom on devices. Swipe up on an app to end it.

Update iOS

- Outdated software might lead to compatibility problems. Check that your iPhone is running the most recent iOS version. iOS 17 is the latest Apple OS.
- Go to **"Settings" > "General" > "Software Update"** and install any available updates.

Reset Camera Settings

- Incorrect camera settings might sometimes cause problems. Restoring camera settings to their default levels might be beneficial.
- Navigate to **"Settings" > "Camera" > "Preserve Settings" > "Reset."**

Clear Camera Cache

- If the problem is cache-related, clearing the camera cache may help. However, unlike Android devices, iPhones do not have a direct option to clean app caches.
- Instead, think about deleting and reinstalling any third-party camera software you've installed.

Free Up Storage Space

- Inadequate storage space on your iPhone might cause performance concerns. To free up storage, delete useless photographs and movies.

Examine Third-Party Camera Apps

- Third-party camera applications may interfere with the default camera app if you have them installed. Uninstall them and check whether the native camera app works properly.

Reset All Settings

- If the issue continues, you can try resetting all of your iPhone's settings. This will not delete your data but will return all settings to their original defaults.
- Navigate to **"Settings" > "General" > "Reset" and then "Reset All Settings."**

Perform a Factory Reset

- If none of the above methods work, a factory reset may be required. This will remove all data on your iPhone, so create a backup of any vital information beforehand.
- Click **"Settings" > "General" > "Reset" > "Erase All Content and Settings."**

Contact Apple Support

If you've tried all of the above instructions and the camera app still crashes, contact Apple Support or visit an Apple Store for assistance. There might be a hardware problem that has to be resolved.

How to troubleshoot iPhone 15 Series Blurry Photos and Videos

It may be quite upsetting to discover that the images and videos you take with your iPhone 15 are continually blurry, distorted, or lack crispness. You most likely desire consistent, clean, high-quality photos. But don't throw away those blurry photos just yet—blurriness is often caused by readily correctable errors or camera setting modifications.

The Most Common Causes of Blurry Photos and Videos

Some common causes of grainy photographs and recordings on your iPhone 15 include:

- **Unsteady hands** - Without optical picture stabilization, even little natural handshakes appear blurry. For stability, enable QuickTake.
- **Moving subjects** - If the shutter speed isn't quick enough, quick-moving subjects might easily blur. Tap to concentrate on a subject.
- **Low illumination** - Poor lighting necessitates a slower shutter speed, which might result in blur. Use the Night mode.
- **Smudges on the lens** - Dust, fingerprints, or debris on the lens impairs a crisp focus. Use a microfiber cloth to gently clean the lens.
- **Digital zooming** - Unlike optical zoom, digital zoom reduces resolution and crispness. Instead of pinching to zoom, move closer.
- **Focus difficulties** - Out-of-focus photos are usually hazy and blurry. Check that auto-focus is turned on, and then touch to focus.

Camera Tips

They include the following:

Change the Camera Settings

While the iPhone 12 and 13 Pro cameras garnered headlines for their high-quality cameras, the 15 and 14 line takes it a step further. The iPhone 15 Pro and 14 Pro both contain a second-generation optical image stabilizer, which allows for better photographs even when your hands move. To get the most out of the new Photonic Engine, go to **Settings > Camera > Formats** and enable **Apple ProRes and 48 megapixels**. With four optical zoom levels and a bigger picture sensor, you can record enormous image sizes.

Enable Apple ProRAW

You can also enable Apple ProRAW, the closest format to professional photography, under the camera options. ProRAW saves raw picture sensor data, providing you with additional options for altering white balance and exposure. In contrast, the JPEG format discards a significant amount of data to compress the file, giving you fewer editing options. While ProRAW photos have excellent resolution and are ideal for editing, keep in mind that they are large files, thus the more storage space you have, the better.

Prepare Phone Storage

If you intend to use Apple ProRAW for all or most of your images, the 15 Pro and 14 Pro provide up to 1TB of storage. This is because an uncooked ProRAW file may be up to 60 MB in size, compared to 9 MB for an adjusted JPEG. You can also purchase more storage space online and upload photographs to iCloud or Google photographs. If you still need more space, consider transferring bigger ProRAW files to a Mac or Windows workstation.

Choose your Style

Other iPhone photography suggestions for beginners include choosing a style and experimenting with various frame rates (fps). If you want to start with simple JPEG images, remember that the greater the frame rate, the smoother the photo will seem. You can change your camera settings to Prioritize Faster Shooting, which improves picture quality, and Lens Correction, which enhances photographs automatically for a more natural look.

Preserve Settings

IPhone photography advice for Instagram often emphasizes the need to preserve camera settings so that you can obtain comparable results in repeated sessions. All you have to do with the iPhone 15 Pro and 14 Pro is choose the Preserve Settings option, which stops the phone from reverting into still camera mode whenever you close the screen. This feature allows you to choose which settings to keep, along with an explanation of each option and how it typically resets.

Use Macro Control

With your settings and storage ready, you can try out various iPhone 15 Pro & 14 Pro camera capabilities including Macro Control. Shooting in Macro mode for small objects, such as up-close nature images or jewelry details, is one of the greatest iPhone photography ideas for beginners. Macro Control activates automatically when you are very near to a subject, as long as you are not in ultrawide 0.5x zoom. When Macro mode is activated, a little symbol appears on the camera app screen. This will result in stunning close-ups and razor-sharp focus for still/live images and movies.

Use Shutter Button

There are many methods for taking images with the clever iPhone 15 Pro & 14 Pro cameras. The shutter button is displayed on the camera screen, or you may take pictures using the phone's volume buttons. Another option is to touch and move the button to the left, which will capture many images for as long as you hold the shutter button down. Tap and hold the shutter or slide it right to lock the recording if you wish to capture a video. Since you can record footage hands-free, this is one of our favorite iPhone photography ideas for TikTok.

Take a Burst

Burst mode on the iPhone 15 and 14 makes it simpler to snap moving objects or to take many shots so you have more to work with. Burst works with both front-facing and rear-facing cameras, sending photographs to a dedicated Burst folder where you can swiftly delete any undesirable photos to free up storage space. Simply touch and move the shutter to the left while holding the button for a flurry of images. The circle around the shutter button shows how many photos were taken in that burst.

Change Exposure

Tap the screen and move up or down to modify the exposure of iPhone 15 Pro and 14 Pro images. With a press and hold on to the appropriate focal area, such as someone's eyes or a major landscape element, you can lock exposure and focus. This guarantees that the settings are maintained throughout the session. One of the best photography tips is to expose the sky while shooting in Apple ProRAW at 48 megapixels for a natural image so that you can bring out information from the shadows later when editing. Remember to hit the little carrot arrow on the top bar to access exposure and flash settings, as well as timing and filter options

Consider Dynamic Island

If you want to shoot professional shots with your iPhone, the Dynamic Island function on the iPhone 15 Pro and 14 Pro is your best chance. In essence, you can keep the camera open and accessible while looking at settings or other iPhone applications. Dynamic Island is useful for verifying warnings and watching recordings as content is being captured.

Use Live Photo

The Live Photo function is still available on the iPhone 15 and 14, and it provides a lengthier snapshot of the three seconds before, during, and after you take a photo. It's like a mini film clip, with many picture frames and views from which you may choose your best final image. From the camera's screen, toggle this setting on and off. For the best results with live iPhone photography tips for portraits, keep the camera motionless and adjust the slider to shift frames.

Include Filters

The iPhone 15 and 14 models include new Portrait mode filters, as well as fan favorites including vibrant, dramatic, and black-and-white. Bring up the picture or video and pick the Edit option to add a filter. Scroll through the filter effects and drag the slider to modify the strength of the filter. To save changes, click **done**; to cancel, select **cancel**.

Auto Edit

Auto editing is often mentioned in iPhone photography recommendations for beginners. The iPhone 15 and 14 have some very advanced picture editing capabilities, and with a single tap, your phone will make automated tweaks to the color, contrast, and exposure. You can also toggle Auto Enhance on and off in iOS 17 settings.

Custom Edit

Auto Enhance and filters are often sufficient for quick picture editing on any iPhone 15 or 14 model. If you want to tweak settings manually, it's simple to make your modifications.

Among the custom edit options are:

- **Exposure** - Adjust the overall brightness or darkness of the image.
- **Highlights** - Illuminate bright areas such as clouds
- **Shadows** - Improve dark shadows on people and structures.
- **Brightness** - Increase saturation and contrast to modify lighting and darkness.
- **Vibrance** - Genuinely enhance colors or mute hues for an aged appearance

Troubleshooting For Sharper Photos

Try these troubleshooting options if your iPhone 15 photos and videos are persistently grainy. This can assist in removing any incorrect and/or irregular settings that are affecting the quality of your iPhone's camera output.

Enable QuickTake Video Stabilization

When you launch your device's camera app, you can use the QuickTake stabilization option to reduce the impression of shaky hand motions when taking photos or recording movies. Simply press and hold the shutter button to activate this mode.

The following are the procedures to activate QuickTake video stabilization on your iPhone 15:

- Launch the **Camera app**.
- Hold down the **Record button**.
- In the upper left corner of the screen, the QuickTake video stabilization icon will appear.
- QuickTake video stabilization is enabled if the icon is green.
- If the symbol is gray, QuickTake video stabilization is turned off.

In the Camera settings, you can also activate or disable QuickTake video stabilization.

Follow these steps to do this:

- Launch the **Settings app**.
- Select **Camera**.
- Select **Stabilization**.
- To activate or disable QuickTake Video Stabilization, toggle the switch.

QuickTake video stabilization aids in the reduction of shakiness in your films. It is very helpful while shooting videos while walking or moving. This will activate the QuickTake stabilization mode, enabling you to shoot crisper and steadier photographs without the need for a tripod or other stabilizing equipment.

Change the Camera Settings

Auto HDR and Smart HDR are features that may assist in increasing illumination clarity and contrast in difficult lighting circumstances.

Here are the procedures for adjusting the Auto HDR and Smart HDR settings on the iPhone 15 camera:

- Launch the **Camera app**.
- In the upper left corner of the screen, tap the **Settings button** (the gear symbol).
- Select **HDR**.

You will be presented with two options:

- **Auto HDR**: This is the default option, and it will activate HDR when it is required.
- **Smart HDR**: This option uses machine learning to automatically adapt the HDR for each photo.

You can also change the following options:

- **HDR off:** Turns off HDR for all photos.
- **Highlight priority**: This option prioritizes retaining highlights in the pictures above maintaining shadow detail.
- **Shadow priority**: This option prioritizes retaining shadow information in the pictures above keeping highlight detail.

These functions function by automatically altering the camera's exposure to capture a broader range of bright and dark regions in an image, resulting in greater detail and sharper focus. By activating these features, you can improve your camera's focus and take better-looking photographs in a variety of lighting circumstances.

Set the Focus

When you're taking a picture, touching the screen of your smartphone will focus the camera on the place you touched. This is particularly critical when capturing moving objects or in low-light situations. You can lock the focus on the subject by holding your finger on the screen until it locks. Tap to set focus is an iPhone 15 feature that lets you manually adjust the camera's focus by touching the screen. This is handy when you want to draw attention to a certain item or area in your photo.

Follow these steps to use tap to set focus:

- Launch the **Camera app**.
- Point the camera at the item or area you want to focus on.

- Tap where you want the emphasis to be on the screen.

The camera will concentrate on the place you touch automatically. You can also change the focus by dragging your finger across the screen. This ensures that your images are clear and focused on the subject you are meant to capture.

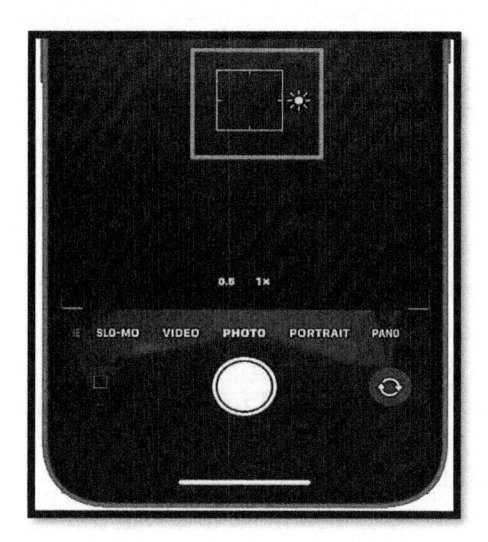

All iPhone 15 models support tapping to set focus. It's a terrific approach to get creative with your images while keeping the attention on the proper subject.

Use Night Mode

Night mode is a camera function that allows you to take higher-quality images in low-light circumstances. It compensates for the lack of light and motion blur that might occur in low-light environments by using sophisticated processing algorithms.

Here's how to use Night Mode on the iPhone 15 camera:

- Launch the **Camera app**.
- Point the camera at the subject you want to capture.
- The Night mode symbol will display in the upper left corner of the screen if the situation is dark.
- To activate Night mode, tap on the symbol.
- The camera will take a longer exposure to collect more light, resulting in a brighter and clearer shot.

You can also change the settings for Night mode:

- **Exposure**: This controls the brightness of the image.
- **Highlights**: This adjusts the brightness of the photo's highlights.
- **Shadows**: This adjusts the brightness of the photo's shadows.

This produces sharper and brighter photos that might have been grainy or too dark to view otherwise.

Avoid using Digital Zoom

The optical zoom lenses use the lens elements to modify the magnification of the picture, preserving the photo's quality. Digital zoom, on the other hand, uses software to magnify the picture, resulting in a loss of sharpness and clarity. To acquire the highest picture quality, it is advised that only optical zoom lenses be used and that the digital zoom feature in the viewfinder be avoided.

Follow these procedures to use the optical zoom lenses on your iPhone 15 camera:

- Launch the **Camera app**.
- Point the camera at the subject you want to capture.
- In the lower right corner of the screen, tap the **Telephoto lens symbol**.
- Then, by moving your finger up and down the screen, you can zoom in and out.

Use a tripod to keep your phone steady

Shaky hands while capturing photographs or videos can often result in blurry images.

- Use a portable tripod or locate a solid, level surface to set your camera on to prevent this.

This will assist in stabilizing your camera and reducing the possibility of motion blur. You will be able to capture crisp and sharp photographs or movies that you will be happy to share with others by doing so.

Clean the Lens of the Rear Camera

Your device's back camera lens is a critical component that captures the photographs or videos you shoot. Dust, oils, and debris may collect on the lens over time, resulting in hazy or distorted pictures.

- It is advised that you carefully wipe the back camera lens using a soft cloth or a lens cleaning kit to avoid this.

- This will keep your camera lens free of dirt and debris, ensuring that your photographs or videos remain crisp and clear.

Your iPhone 15 is capable of taking amazingly crisp, print-worthy photos and smooth videos with experience and changing settings for your shooting situations. Remember to stay still!

IPhone 15 Camera Not Focusing Issues

What if you go on a vacation and your new iPhone stops taking pictures? That will be frustrating if, after paying so much money, we end up with the iPhone 15 series camera lens blurry problem. Sometimes we find ourselves in this painful situation as a result of our miscalculation.

Dirty External Lens

Is your iPhone's camera constantly blurring and deblurring? After a long period, the lens may get filthy, or if your iPhone survives a dusty environment, you will discover an iPhone with a blurry camera. This camera problem on the iPhone might be caused by dirt, smudges, or dust. Since this is the case, the camera is unable to identify the object and fails to focus. However, our initial thought was to remove the dirt with our fingers, but this was not the best option; instead, use a soft cloth to clean the iPhone's camera lens.

Examine the camera and other settings listed below:

- **Storage is an issue**: Your iPhone's storage capacity is insufficient to shoot and save HD photos. Your iPhone will then snap and save the optimized version of the shot. That indicates you've been resold as blurry.
- **Disable Reduce White Point:** Go to your iPhone's settings and test your camera to see what's different in your situation. Go to the **Settings app**, then to **General**, then to **Accessibility**, then to **Display Accommodations**, and finally to **Disable Reduce White Point**.

Remove the Case

Assume you have an iPhone 15 Pro Max focusing problem with near objects. Eventually, some malfunctioning cases cause you so many troubles. So have a look at the casing or remove it for a moment and use the camera to check whether the lens is operating correctly.

Assist your iPhone in focusing

Normally, the iPhone is capable of autofocusing; however, because you are experiencing blurry camera issues with your iPhone, assist the iPhone in focusing. To do so, launch the camera app, aim the camera at the item, and touch the screen. The item will be recognized when you touch the camera screen.

Restart the Camera app

Still, if your iPhone camera isn't focusing, try this troubleshooting method. If a brief software problem is interfering with the iPhone camera, forcibly closing and re-launching the camera app will resolve the issue.

The steps:

- Pause by swiping up from the bottom of the screen.
- You will now see the apps that are operating in the background. Swiping up on a certain app closes them. This mostly aids in the removal of the temporary camera app problem and will address the iPhone 15 camera constantly focusing or blinking issue.

Force Restart iPhone

Since re-launching the camera did not work for certain users, the only option is to forcibly restart the iPhone. The system reboot may resolve all iPhone issues.

- First, press and hold the Volume Up button.
- Press and hold the **Volume Down button** for a few seconds.
- Hold down the **Side button** until the Apple logo appears on the screen.

DFU Restore

If the iPhone camera lens is still blurry, you can decide to attempt this probable remedy to resolve the strange problem. You should make a backup of your device as a precaution to prevent data loss.

Here's how to do a DFU restore on an iPhone:

- Close all applications on your computer and start iTunes.
- Turn off the iPhone.
- Connect the iPhone to the PC.

- Press and hold the Side button for 3 seconds.
- Next, press and hold the **Volume Down button** while keeping your finger on the Side button. For 10 seconds, hold down the **Volume Down and Side buttons**.
- Keep the Volume Down button down for more than 5 seconds. If you see the Plugin iTunes screen on your iPhone, you must redo steps 4-6 since the procedure failed.
- After successfully entering DFU mode, the iPhone screen will stay dark. Furthermore, the PC will display that iTunes has recognized the device.
- All that remains is for you to follow the on-screen directions and finish the procedure.

Get Apple Support

If nothing else works to resolve your iPhone camera lens difficulties, you should contact Apple Support. There will most likely be a problem with the iPhone's camera's hardware; they can only solve this. Make an appointment at the Apple Store to save time.

How to fix the camera flash not working

There are a variety of reasons why your iPhone's flash is disabled. However, when this happens, you are unable to use your iPhone's flashlight. You cannot snap images with the flash since the flash mode will not function no matter what you do. If you find yourself in this scenario, the tips outlined below might be of great assistance to you.

Errors Caused by "iPhone Flash is Disabled"

The flash on an iPhone is deactivated for one of two reasons. These two arguments are as follows.

- The iPhone battery is low and needs to be charged before you can use the flash."

> **Flash is Disabled**
>
> The iPhone battery is low and needs to be charged before you can use the flash.
>
> OK

If your iPhone's battery is going low and there isn't much electricity left in the phone, it will turn off the flash to save battery charge. The flash will stay disabled until and unless your phone is fully charged.

- The iPhone needs to cool down before you can use the flash.

> **Flash is Disabled**
>
> The iPhone needs to cool down before you can use the flash.
>
> OK

When the temperature of your iPhone exceeds a particular threshold, the flash is deactivated and the iPhone has to cool down. The flash will stay switched off as long as your iPhone has not cooled down to normal operating temperatures.

How to Repair an iPhone Flashlight That Isn't Working

Before you go to a specialist to replace your broken flashlight, consider these alternatives that will save you time and money.

They include the following:

Close the Camera application

Both the flashlight and the camera are powered by ED light. This implies that you can't use the rear flashlight and the camera at the same time. To use your flashlight, you must first shut the camera app if it is open.

Charge your iPhone first

If your iPhone's battery is almost depleted, the iPhone flashlight will not function. As a result, before using the flashlight, make sure your iPhone has enough battery life. You should also make certain that "**Low Power Mode**" is not activated, since this prohibits you from using the flashlight. To see whether the mode is activated, go to Settings > Battery.

Remove the iPhone Cover if Covered

If your iPhone is covered with an opaque cover, it signifies that the flashlight lens is obscured. Check that the iPhone case is not obscuring the flashlight. If it is obstructing the flash, it should be removed.

Turn the Camera flash ON and then OFF

Your iPhone Flashlight may fail to function since it is most likely trapped in the camera app. If this is the case, open the Camera app and, in the **Video section**, tap the **flash icon**. Set the flash on and off to verify that it is closed before attempting to open the flashlight on your iPhone.

Restart your iPhone

Minor flaws might create difficulties with your iPhone, stopping it from functioning properly. Simply restarting your iPhone is a simple tip that you should always use. A simple restart may resolve a variety of issues with your iPhone. You can do so by going to **Settings > General > Shut Down**. Allow your iPhone one minute before restarting it.

Check and Install Updates

Pending software upgrades on your iPhone might create issues that prohibit the flashlight from working.

To check for updates, go to:

- Go to **Settings**.
- Navigate to the **General tab** and choose **Software Update**.
- Select "**Download and Install**" from the menu.

Reset iPhone Settings

You can restore factory settings on your iPhone by resetting its settings, but no data will be lost. To do this, go to **Settings > General > Reset > Reset all Settings**. Tap on the reset button to confirm the pop-up. You can then attempt to test the flashlight to see whether it works.

Force Restart iPhone

A force restart might assist you in resolving the flashlight not functioning issue. To achieve this, first briefly push the **Volume up button**, then the **Volume down button**, and lastly long-press the side button until the logo appears. If none of the suggestions above work, then your iPhone most likely has a hardware issue that only a specialist can resolve.

Toggle Low Power Mode on and off

Low Power Mode is an iPhone function that allows you to prolong the life of your phone's battery while it is running low on power. This function disables some things on your iPhone, and you should try turning it on and off to see if it solves your flash issue.

- On your iPhone, go to **Settings > Battery** and enable **Low Power Mode**.

- After a minute, disable the function.

Optimize battery charging by turning on and off

Optimize Battery Charging is an iOS 17 function that promises to help your iPhone's battery last longer. To check whether this option helps your problem, toggle it on and off.

- On your iPhone, go to **Settings > Battery > Battery Health** and activate **Optimized Battery Charging**.
- After roughly a minute, disable the function.

How to Fix a Non-Working Camera

Here are the steps:

- Remove any cover case that may be interfering with the iPhone's ability to take images.
- Take a photo to test the camera. Then switch to the front or back camera and snap another shot to see whether either or both cameras are still working properly.
- If the image is blurry, use a microfiber cloth to wipe the front and rear lenses. If you see any dirt within the lens, contact Apple for assistance.
- Start your iPhone again.

How to Troubleshoot Night Mode Issues

The iPhone 15 series, like prior generations, has a night mode that is supposed to take better low-light shots and minimize noise in your photos. If you're having difficulties using Night mode, follow these steps to diagnose and perhaps resolve the issue:

Ensure that your software is up to date

Ensure that the iOS (iOS 17) on your iPhone is up to date. Apple often releases software upgrades that incorporate camera features and performance enhancements.

Examine the Camera Settings

Launch the Camera app and toggle on Night mode. You can enable or disable it from the Camera interface.

Stable Support

Night mode demands a steady hand to function properly. To eliminate camera shaking, use a tripod, a steady surface, or a function like the countdown timer.

Clean the Lens of the Camera

Wipe the camera lens with a clean, soft cloth to remove any smudges or grime that may be compromising the clarity of your images.

Avoid Using Extremely Low Lighting

Night mode works best in relatively low-light circumstances. Night mode may not operate properly in excessively dark environments.

Experiment with Exposure Time

In the Camera app, hit the **Night mode icon** to manually change the exposure time using the slider. Experiment with different exposure periods to find which works best for your circumstances.

Use a Flash

In certain low-light circumstances, employing the flash instead of Night mode may be more effective. When shooting images in very dark conditions, enable the flash in the Camera app.

Composition and Focus

Make sure your camera is correctly focused and that your photo is nicely composed. If the camera is having difficulty focusing or the composition is congested, night mode may be less effective.

Take Multiple Photos

Night mode may take a series of images with varying exposures and then combine them to get a better image. Taking many photos of the same scene may sometimes provide superior results.

Reboot your iPhone

Restarting your iPhone will sometimes repair temporary software faults that are impacting Night mode.

Examine for Hardware Issues

If you're still having problems, there might be a hardware issue with the camera. Consider calling Apple Support or visiting an Apple Store or authorized service facility in this scenario.

Speak with Apple Support

If everything else fails and you're still having problems with Night mode, contact Apple Support for more help or potential hardware diagnostics. Remember that Night mode may not always give excellent results in every setting, since it is affected by a variety of elements such as light intensity, movement, and composition.

How to Correct Inconsistent Portrait Mode

Adjustments and troubleshooting may be required to correct uneven portrait mode results on the iPhone 15 series.

Here are the steps to correct inconsistent portrait mode:

Clean the Camera Lens

Check that your camera's lens is clean and clear of smudges or dirt. Clean the lens lightly using a microfiber cloth.

Provide Adequate Lighting

Portrait mode performs best in well-lit environments. To prevent inconsistencies, make sure your subject is well-illuminated, ideally with natural light.

iOS Update

To check for iOS updates, go to **"Settings" > "General" > "Software Update."** Updating your iOS might help you overcome software-related difficulties.

Reset Camera Settings

If you've made major changes to your camera settings, portrait mode can be affected. To reset the camera's settings, go to **"Settings"** > **"Camera"** > **"Preserve Settings"** > **"Reset."**

Adjust the focus and exposure

Tap and hold on the subject you want to focus on while in the Camera app. This may aid in calibrating the camera and improving the accuracy of the background blur.

Adjust the Depth Control

Once you've taken a portrait picture, access it in the Photos app. The background blur may be adjusted using the "**Edit**" option and the Depth Control slider.

Examine for Conflicting Objects

Check for any things that are too near to the subject and might interfere with the depth-sensing technology. Remove any possible impediments.

Maintain the Proper Distance

Make sure you're standing at the proper distance from your subject for the best results. The depth-sensing technology on the iPhone works best within a specified range.

Avoid cluttered backgrounds

Portrait mode is more effective with plain backgrounds. It should be avoided in circumstances with complicated or busy backdrops.

Experiment with Lighting Effects

Portrait Mode on the iPhone after capturing the shot, you can change the lighting effects. To improve your picture, experiment with various lighting effects.

Use a tripod or other kind of stabilization

Inconsistent outcomes might be caused by shaky hands. To keep the camera steady, use a tripod or a firm surface if feasible.

Take Several Shots

Portrait mode isn't always great the first time you use it. Take many shots to maximize your chances of attaining the desired outcome.

Use Third-Party Apps

If you continue to have problems with the default camera app, think about using third-party camera applications that provide more sophisticated controls and settings for portrait shooting.

Get in touch with Apple Support

If the issue remains after you've done everything else, call Apple Support or visit an Apple Store for assistance. There might be a hardware problem that requires expert assistance.

How to solve live photos not playing

If your iPhone 15 series isn't playing Live Photos, you may attempt a few troubleshooting methods to fix the problem. Live Photos are an entertaining and engaging feature that records a few seconds of video and audio before and after shooting a photo.

Check that Live Photos is enabled

- On your iPhone, launch the **Camera app.**
- Make sure the Live Photo function is turned on. This can be found in the Camera app's toolbar. A round symbol with concentric rings represents it.

Examine Storage Space

- A lack of storage capacity might have an impact on the operation of Live Photos. Check that your device has adequate free space.
- Go to **"Settings" > "General" > "iPhone Storage"** to see how much storage space you have available.

Examine the Camera Settings

In the camera settings, Live Photos can sometimes be turned off. To confirm this:

- Launch the **Camera app.**
- To access camera settings, swipe up on the screen.
- Make sure that Live Photos is set to "**Auto**" or "**On**."

Reboot your iPhone

Minor software issues are often resolved with a quick restart. Hold down the power button until you see the "**slide to power off**" slider appear. Turn off your device and then on again.

Update iOS

- Ensure that your iPhone is running the most recent version of iOS. Compatibility concerns might arise from outdated software.
- Go to "**Settings**" > "**General**" > "**Software Update**" to check for and install any available updates.

Force Restart

If Live Photos are still not functioning, attempt a force restart to fix any underlying software issues. The procedures for forcibly restarting your iPhone 15 may differ significantly based on the model. In general, it entails swiftly pushing and releasing the volume up and volume down buttons, followed by holding down the side (or power) button until the Apple logo shows.

Reset All Settings

- If none of the above procedures work, try resetting all settings. This will not remove your data, but it will return all settings to their default configuration.
- Navigate to "**Settings**" > "**General**" > "**Reset**" > "**Reset All Settings.**"

Restoring from Backup

If the problem persists, you may need to restore your iPhone from a backup. Check that you have a recent backup, then:

- Navigate to "**Settings**" > "**General**" > "**Reset**" > "**Erase All Content and Settings.**" After deleting your iPhone, you can restore it from a backup.

Get in touch with Apple Support

If Live Photos are still not functioning after doing all of the above procedures, the problem may be more complicated and need the aid of Apple Support. If necessary, they may give more instructions or recommend hardware diagnostics.

IPhone Continuity Camera Isn't Working

Are you ecstatic about the new iPhone continuity camera but having trouble getting it to work?

What exactly is a Continuity Camera?

Apple has recently introduced Sonoma, its newest operating system. The all-new Continuity Camera is one of the release's brightest stars. You may now utilize your iPhone as a camera on your Mac. However, if you attempt to use your iPhone and Continuity Camera in a web browser, particularly for online recordings, you can encounter some difficulties.

How to Repair Chrome's Continuity Camera

Many people who are attempting to use Continuity Camera in Chrome as the video input claim that the option is no longer available after upgrading to macOS Sonoma.

To correct this, just follow these steps:

- In Google Chrome, click the three dots and choose **Settings**.
- Select **Privacy and Security**, followed by Site Settings.
- Navigate down to Camera. When you click Camera, you'll find that you have a selection of cameras, but your iPhone is most likely not showing up, even if Continuity Camera is functioning in other apps.
- To make it appear, use another app that allows you to use your iPhone as a camera, like FaceTime.
- In FaceTime, go to the Video menu and choose your iPhone from the camera.

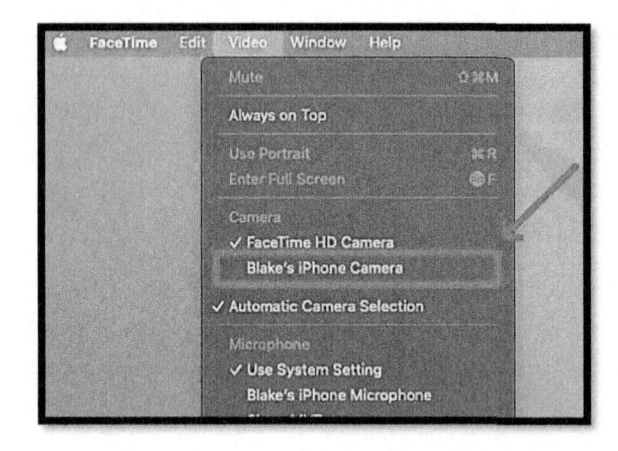

- Restart Google Chrome to see the option (you may also need to restart your computer during this procedure).
- Return to the three dots. Go back to settings and choose Privacy and Security Site settings. Move down to Camera.
- In this panel, your iPhone should display as a camera option.

Frequently Asked Questions

1. How do you solve camera crashes on your iPhone 15 Series?
2. How do you solve blurry photos and videos on your iPhone?
3. How do you troubleshoot your iPhone to provide sharper photos?
4. How do you fix the camera flash not working?
5. How do you solve issues with night mode?
6. How do you correct inconsistent portrait mode?
7. How do you solve live photos not playing on your iPhone 15 Series?

CONCLUSION

Apple has recently unveiled the highly anticipated iPhone 15 Series, which boasts an array of noteworthy advancements in camera technology. Enthusiasts can expect to be captivated by the enhanced camera capabilities and the introduction of innovative features integrated into the camera system. First off, the iPhone 15 and iPhone 15 Plus are equipped with a dual-slanted Main camera system, a feature that has been previously observed in the iPhone 13 mini and iPhone 14 models. Apple has chosen to retain a consistent design across both the iPhone 15 and iPhone 15 Plus models, while significantly enhancing the camera specifications, surpassing those of previous iterations. The Pro models, in contrast, offer a substantial array of enhancements compared to the initial two iterations.

The advanced camera technology featured on the iPhone 15 and iPhone 15 plus enables users to capture their daily experiences and cherished memories, enhancing the value and appeal of their past moments for viewers, particularly when shared with friends and family. Featuring a quad-pixel sensor and 100 percent Focus Pixels for swift and accurate focusing, the 48MP Main camera adeptly captures high-quality photographs and videos, effectively preserving intricate details. Using the features of computational photography, the Main camera offers users a cutting-edge 24MP super-high-resolution option, delivering exceptional image quality while maintaining a practical file size suitable for both archiving and sharing purposes. The iPhone dual-camera system now incorporates a novel 2x Telephoto option, which seamlessly combines hardware and software to offer users three distinct optical-quality zoom levels: 0.5x, 1x, and 2x.

The Pro series features a dedicated 48MP Main camera that offers customers an expanded range of options. Notably, it introduces a new 24MP super-high-resolution preset, which delivers exceptional picture quality while maintaining a manageable file size, making it ideal for both preserving and sharing images. The Main camera allows users to seamlessly switch between three commonly used focal lengths, namely 24 mm, 28 mm, and 35 mm. additionally; users have the flexibility to designate one of these focal lengths as their preferred default option. In addition to capturing 48MP ProRAW images, the Main camera also provides the capability to capture 48MP HEIF photographs at a resolution that is four times higher. The iPhone 15 Pro boasts a substantial 3x Telephoto camera, whereas the iPhone 15 Pro Max showcases an unprecedented optical zoom capability, reaching an impressive 5x at 120 mm, setting a new standard for iPhone devices. The recently introduced Telephoto camera featured in the iPhone 15 Pro Max is exceptionally well-suited for capturing close-up shots, engaging in wildlife photography, and seizing action-packed moments from afar. The device boasts a distinctive tetraprism design, incorporating an advanced optical image stabilization and autofocus 3D sensor-shift module. This cutting-edge technology represents Apple's most formidable stabilization capability to date.

INDEX

1

10-bit files with great sensor data retention., 51
12-megapixel telephoto lens., 5
12MP TrueDepth camera, 6
12MP Ultra Wide camera, 4

2

24mm lens equivalent, 5

4

48-megapixel camera, 5
48MP HEIF images, 5
48MP resolutions, 5

A

A lack of storage capacity, 179
A pop-up menu, 68, 72
absence of using portrait mode, 4
Absorb bounces and shakes with your body., 19
access the Camera app, 7, 74
Accessibility, 105, 116, 169
activate Face ID access, 103
Add depth-of-field to your videos, 23
Add the screen recorder to the control center, 71
Additional controls and settings, 13
additional options available for LOG encoding, 6
Adds a blue tint to the vivid filter., 82
Adequate Time, 39
Adjust the Depth Control, 178
adjust the exposure level, 13
Adjust the focus and exposure, 178
Adjust the Length, 128
Adjust the screen brightness and color on the iPhone, 105
Adjust the sharing options, 91
Adjustments and troubleshooting, 177
advanced 3D sensor shift optical image stabilization,, 6

advanced low-noise circuitry, 61
advanced optical image stabilization, 183
after shooting a photo., 179
After Taking a Photo, 153
AirDrop, 21, 89, 90, 91, 94, 155
Albums, 85, 89, 91, 96, 98, 101, 102, 103, 125, 130, 132, 135, 136, 137, 138, 141
Align the viewfinder, 64
All Photos, 86, 87, 91, 94, 101, 132
An album, 123
An iPhone 15 Pro or 15 Pro Max, 23
another FaceTime call, 113
Apple Headphone, 61
Apple Headphone Jack Adapter, 61
Apple logo, 170, 180
Apple Store for assistance, 160, 179
Apple's advanced 3D sensor, 6
Apple's advanced 3D sensor shift optical, 6
Apple's cloud storage service, 154
Apple's flagship phone series, 23
Apple's latest offering, 3
Apple's portrait mode, 6
Apply a blue tint to the Dramatic filter, 82
Aspect Ratio Grid, 142
aspiring home cinematographers, 47
Assist your iPhone in focusing, 170
attaining the desired outcome, 179
Auto Edit, 164
autofocus 3D sensor-shift, 183
autofocus 3D sensor-shift module, 183
Automatically adjust the screen brightness, 105
available photography modes, 13
Avoid cluttered backgrounds, 178
Avoid using Digital Zoom, 168
Avoid Using Extremely Low Lighting, 176

B

Backup iPhone Memory Videos Using iCloud, 129
Backup to iCloud, 154
Backup your photos locally, 156
Basic Exposure and Shooting Techniques, 32
Before Taking a Photo, 153

Before you start recording, put your phone on airplane mode., 21
Better Exposure, 33
Better Video Quality, 30
better-looking photo, 20
Blue Flare Anamorphic, 57
blurring and deblurring, 169
boasting a focal length, 4, 6
breathtaking clarity, 30
Brightness, 105, 106, 107, 164
bringing one iPhone close to another, 91
Browse photos in your library, 86
bumps or wobbles, 32
Burst Photos, 138

C

Call again, 113
calling Apple Support, 177
camera angles, 42
Camera app, 7, 10, 17, 18, 21, 25, 26, 27, 28, 30, 34, 40, 42, 52, 53, 55, 64, 73, 74, 75, 78, 79, 81, 82, 83, 144, 145, 152, 153, 156, 170, 173, 176, 178, 179
Camera application, 7, 15
Camera Application, 58
camera option, 182
camera settings, 13, 28, 49, 73, 149, 159, 162, 178, 179
Camera Settings, 28, 30, 161, 165
camera symbol, 34, 96
camera technology, 182, 183
Camera Tips, 161
Camera viewfinder area, 75
camera's lens, 177
camera's shutter, 14
capability to capture images, 5
captivating animation, 11
captivating animation feature, 11
capture 48MP HEIF photographs, 183
Capture a Still Image from a Video on an iPhone, 22
capture of 4K ProRes video at 60fps, 6
capture Slo-mo films, 40
capture time-lapse videos, 39
capture video footage in ProRes, 16
capture video footage in ProRes format, 16
captures high-quality photographs, 183
captures high-quality photographs and videos, 183
captures stunning selfies, 4

capturing 48MP ProRAW, 183
capturing 48MP ProRAW images, 183
capturing a video, 20
capturing images, 5, 16
capturing images with a significant sense of depth, 5
capturing photos or videos, 13, 17
capturing shots, 3
Change Cameras, 113
Change Exposure, 163
Change how photos appear in an album, 141
Change the angle of your camera, 42
Change the Auto FPS settings, 37
Change the camera's video, 37
Change the capture time, 149
change the exposure time, 176
Change the file format, 91
Change the size of the text., 97
Change to 4K Resolution, 30
Changing the Title, 127
Charge your iPhone first, 173
Check and Install Updates, 173
Choose a font., 97
Choose a spot with plenty of natural light, 19
choose the **Trash icon**, 88
Choose your Style, 162
Choosing Your Memoji, 114
Cinematic, 4, 16, 20, 23, 37, 38, 64, 65
cinematic and slo-mo modes, 13
Cinematic mode, 4, 16, 20, 37, 64
Clean the Camera Lens, 177
Clean the Lens of the Camera, 176
Clean the Lens of the Rear Camera, 168
Clear Camera Cache, 160
Close Background Apps, 159
compact TRRS microphone, 58
compatible models, 18
Composition, 32, 176
Composition and Focus, 176
computational capabilities, 4
CONCLUSION, 182
configuring video color, 6
Connect a camera, 93
Connect an iPhone, 93
Connect the iPhone to the PC., 170
Consider Dynamic Island, 163
Consider the video sound, 42
Contact Apple Support, 160
Continuity Camera, 181

continuous manual button, 11
Control Center, 27, 71, 72, 94, 105, 107, 155, 157
Converts to plain black and white., 82
Crane for Camera and iPhone, 59
Create a Memoji, 113
Create a Photographic Style, 74
Create a standard photographic style, 74
Create a video that has a slow-motion effect., 23
create high-quality commercial movies, 18

'

'**Create Photo Memory**', 126

C

Creating a Memory for a Person, 125
Creating a Memory from an Album or Day/ Month, 124
Crop your video, 46
Cropping photos, 104
Custom Edit, 164
cutting-edge technology, 183

D

default configuration, 180
Default photo filters and how they transform photos, 81
default setting, 13, 78
Deity V-Mic D4 Duo Microphone Portable Voice Recorder, 60
Delete, 71, 87, 89, 132, 136, 137, 138, 141
device's extensive pixel, 5
DFU Restore, 170
different exposure periods, 176
Digital zooming, 161
Dirty External Lens, 169
disable HDR Video, 29, 38
Disable Reduce White Point, 169
Disable the "View Outside Frame" option, 31
discussion on cameras, 10
displaying brighter highlights, 31
distinctive tetraprism design, 183
Do not send your videos to your computer via text or email, 21
dog's joyful activities, 32

download and install the **Frame Grabber software**, 22
dramatic contrasts, 31
Dramatic Cool, 82
Dramatic Warm, 82
During a FaceTime call, 113, 116

E

Editing a Memory, 126
Editing Pre-Made iPhone Memories, 119
Effect in Photos, 146
either ProRAW or HEIF formats, 5
emphasized iOS's privacy features, 102
enable Action Mode,, 48
Enable iCloud Backup, 154
enable iCloud photos, 91
Enable My Photo Stream, 155
Enable ProRes, 54
enable ProRes capture, 56
Enable **Scheduled**., 107
Enable Stabilization, 32
Enable two-factor authentication, 156
encompassing 4K video capture, 4
End the Recording, 72
engage in FaceTime calls, 4
enhanced photography experience, 58
enhanced sharpness, 4
enjoy the cinematic mode, 6
enlarges the image, 19
Ensure that your software is up to date, 175
Erase All Content and Settings.", 160, 180
Errors Caused by "iPhone Flash is Disabled", 171
Examine for Conflicting Objects, 178
Examine for Hardware Issues, 177
Examine Storage Space, 179
Examine the Camera Settings, 175, 179
Examine the EXIF data, 22
Examine Third-Party Camera Apps, 160
excellent time-lapse programs, 39
exceptional device, 58
exceptional picture quality, 183
excessively dark environments., 176
Experiment with Exposure Time, 176
Experiment with Lighting Effects, 178
Experiment with Time-Lapse in Night Mode, 37
Export Unmodified Original, 93
expose the photo., 20
Exposure, 32, 164, 168, 176

EXPOSURE, 73
external storage device, 93

F

Face ID or your device's PIN code., 102
FACETIME, 110
FaceTime calls, 115, 116, 118
FaceTime session, 114, 116, 118
FaceTime video call, 111, 112, 115
fascinating natural landscapes, 40
favorite iPhone photography ideas for TikTok, 163
feature streamlines, 6
features of computational photography, 183
featuring a 12-megapixel ultra-wide lens, 5
Featuring a quad-pixel sensor, 183
few additional modes, 14
filming great handheld videos, 19
Final Cut Pro, 17
Flipping Photos, 104
focal lengths, 13, 183
focus and exposure boxes, 20
Focus difficulties, 161
Force Restart, 170, 174, 180
formidable stabilization, 183
formidable stabilization capability, 183
Frame Grabber app, 22
frames per second, 4, 6, 16, 30, 37, 40, 51, 55
framing your shot, 18
Free Up Storage Space, 160
Frequently Asked Questions, 33, 50, 72, 84, 109, 118, 142, 158, 182
From a text message, 92
From an email, 92
From an iCloud link, 92
full-quality photographs, 91
functionality of capturing burst photos, 10
fundamental concepts, 13

G

Get Apple Support, 171
Get in touch with Apple Support, 179, 180
GETTING STARTED, 3
Go to Settings on your iPhone., 41
Google Chrome, 181
GoPro devices., 62

greater level of zoom, 5

H

harmonizing the colors, 33
HDR, 4, 6, 10, 16, 17, 20, 25, 28, 29, 30, 31, 38, 47, 52, 64, 145, 165, 166
Hidden album, 102, 103
High Dynamic Range, 17, 20, 30
Highlights, 164, 168
highly anticipated iPhone 15 Series, 182
highly-rated free app, 96
high-resolution images, 3
How can I disable the timer on my iPhone 15 camera?, 79
How do you add or remove photos within memory?, 142
How do you add text to your images?, 109
How do you adjust cinematic mode focus post-shoot?, 72
How do you adjust depth control and portrait lighting?, 158
How do you adjust focus and exposure?, 84
How do you adjust your screen brightness?, 109
How do you align your image using a grid?, 84
How do you capture an image in night mode?, 158
How do you capture photos from a video?, 33
How do you change the camera modes?, 33
How do you change the memory mix?, 142
How do you choose a photographic style?, 84
How do you convert normal video to slo-mo?, 50
How do you correct inconsistent portrait mode?, 182
How do you create a folder in photos?, 142
How do you create a link to a FaceTime call?, 118
How do you create a memory from an album?, 142
How do you create a memory movie on your iPhone 15 Series?, 142
How do you cut a clip out of a video?, 72
How do you delete unnecessary photo albums?, 142
How do you fix the camera flash not working?, 182
How do you hide and access your images?, 109
How do you import and export videos?, 109
How do you make and receive a FaceTime call?, 118
How do you move an existing album into a folder?, 142
How do you navigate through the Photos app?, 109
How do you organize images in your album?, 142
How do you protect the memories of a video?, 142

How do you record a slow-motion video?, 50
How do you record a video message and leave a voicemail on FaceTime?, 118
How do you record cinematic videos?, 72
How do you record your iPhone screen?, 72
How do you recover deleted images?, 109
How do you scan QR codes?, 158
How do you set up FaceTime?, 118
How do you set up Photographic styles?, 84
How do you share and delete photos?, 109
How do you share your favorite memories?, 142
How do you shoot macro video in slow motion or in time-lapse?, 158
How do you solve blurry photos and videos on your iPhone?, 182
How do you solve camera crashes on your iPhone 15 Series?, 182
How do you solve issues with night mode?, 182
How do you solve live photos not playing on your iPhone 15 Series?, 182
How do you speed up a slow-motion video?, 50
How do you take a photo using a filter?, 84
How do you take a picture or record a video?, 33
How do you trim a video?, 72
How do you troubleshoot your iPhone to provide sharper photos?, 182
How do you turn photos into portraits after shooting?, 158
How do you turn the camera flash on or off?, 84
How do you use a timer on your iPhone 15 Series?, 84
How do you use and customize action mode?, 50
How do you use automatic macro switching control?, 158
How do you use Memoji on FaceTime?, 118
How Does Night Mode Function?, 148
How does the iPhone camera timer work?, 79
How photos and videos are organized in Photos, 85
How slow motion works on iPhone, 40
How to add a filter to a photo you've already taken, 81
How to Add an Album to a Folder, 133
How to add and remove photos within memory, 127
How to add text to your pictures, 95
How to adjust exposure, 46
How to adjust focus and exposure, 75
How to Adjust the Shutter Volume, 26
How to align your photo using a grid, 82
How to blur the background, 117

How to Capture Log Footage, 23
How to Capture Log Footage on an iPhone 15 Pro, 23
How to Capture Log Footage on an iPhone 15 Pro Versions, 23
How to Change a Photo Album's Cover Photo, 135
How to Change iPhone Time Lapse Settings, 39
How to change the camera modes, 22
How to Change the Cover Photo of an Album in Photos, 135
How to change the lighting, 105
How to change the lighting and color scheme, 105
How to change the memory mix, 121
How to convert normal video to slo-mo, 42
How to Correct Inconsistent Portrait Mode, 177
How to Create a Folder in Photos, 132
How to create a link to a FaceTime call, 115
How to create a memory movie, 119
How to Create an Album in Photos, 130
How to create new albums in the Photos app, 130
How to crop, 104
How to crop, flip, and rotate photos, 104
How to customize Action Mode, 49
How to customize the main camera lens, 29
How to cut a clip out of a video, 70
How to cut a video on iPhone into parts, 69
How to Delete and Share Photos, 87
How to Enable iCloud Photos, 154
How to Fix a Non-Working Camera, 175
How to fix the camera flash not working, 171
How to hide photos, 102
How to identify and remove identical-looking images, 138
How to include background sounds on a FaceTime call, 116
How to make a photo part of your favorite, 100
How to make and receive a FaceTime call, 111
How to Make Your Slow Motion Video Pop, 42
How to Move an Existing Album into a Folder on iPhone, 134
How to navigate through the Photos app, 85
How to Open the Camera, 6
How to Organize Photos in an Album, 137
How to quickly rename iPhone Screenshots, 140
How to record a QuickTake video, 34
How to record a slow-motion video, 40
How to record cinematic video, 64
How to record in ProRes on iPhone 15 Series, 54
How to record the screen, 71

How to Recover Deleted Pictures and Videos, 97
How to Recover Deleted Pictures and Videos from the Photos App, 97
How to remove objects in photos, 63
How to Rename Photos on iPhone, 140
How to Repair an iPhone Flashlight That Isn't Working, 172
How to Repair Chrome's Continuity, 181
How to revert an adjusted image, 108
How to scan QR codes, 156
How to set a timer on iPhone 15 without Burst?, 80
How to set up FaceTime, 110
How to Set up Photographic Styles, 74
How to share your favorite memories, 121
How to share your screen on a FaceTime call, 117
How to shoot a slow-motion video with your iPhone, 42
How to Shoot Macro Photos on an iPhone 15 Series, 143
How to shoot macro video in time-lapse or slow-motion, 144
How to Shoot Video on an iPhone, 18
How to Shoot Videos, 64
How to slow down your video, 45
How to Solve Camera Crashes, 159
How to solve live photos not playing, 179
How to speed up a slow-motion video, 44
How to start a FaceTime Audio, 115
How to start a FaceTime Audio/Video call from messages, 115
How to take a photo with a filter, 80
How to take a picture, 17, 145, 148
How to take a picture or record a video, 17
How to Take Photos from a Video, 21
How to trim a video, 67
How to trim, crop, and straighten your slow-motion video, 45
How to troubleshoot iPhone 15 Series, 160
How to troubleshoot iPhone 15 Series Blurry Photos, 160
How to troubleshoot iPhone 15 Series Blurry Photos and Videos, 160
How to Troubleshoot Night Mode Issues, 175
How to turn on live captions, 116
How to Turn Photos into Portraits after Shooting, 145
How to turn the camera flash on or off, 75
How to unhide or view hidden photos, 103
How to upload your photos and keep them safe, 154
How to use a timer, 77
How to use action mode, 47
How to use automatic macro switching control, 144
How to use depth control, 153
How to Use iMovie to Split and Rearrange Clips, 69
How to Use Live Text, 150, 152
How to use live text with the camera, 150
How to use Memoji on FaceTime, 113
How to Use Night Mode, 149
How to use the iPhone camera app to capture a shot with a filter, 81
How to zoom in and zoom out, 26

I

iCloud images, 154
iCloud photos, 87, 130
image on a specific subject, 5
Image or Save Image as PNG, 97
impacting Night mode., 177
implemented notable enhancements, 4
Import and export photos, 92
Import and Export Videos, 92
Import selected items, 93
improve visual quality, 31
improved user experience characterized, 4
In contrast to the original, 63
Include Filters, 164
inclusion of the A17 Pro chip, 6
incorporating an advanced optical, 183
Increases contrast, 81
Increases the shadows and decreases the highlights, 82
independent attribute, 4
initial capture, 4
innovative programmable Action Button, 10
innovative tetraprism design, 6
Insert an SD memory card, 93
Instagram or Facebook Live, 62
Instagram or Facebook Live sessions, 62
Instagram Posts, 69
Instagram Stories, 69
Install and launch the Phonto app on your iPhone., 96
Instead of pinching to zoom, move your phone closer, 19
intricate controls, 13
introduced Telephoto camera featured, 183
INTRODUCTION, 1

introduction of Smart HDR 5, 6
introduction of Smart HDR 5 and notable enhancements, 6
iOS devices, 58
iOS Update, 177
iPhone 13 Pro, 61, 143
iPhone 13 Pro Max, 61, 143
iPhone 14 Pro, 5, 52, 143
iPhone 15 - On-screen controls, 11
IPhone 15 and iPhone 15 Plus, 3
IPhone 15 Camera Not Focusing Issues, 169
iPhone 15 Pro, 5, 6, 8, 12, 16, 18, 23, 24, 29, 34, 51, 52, 55, 57, 72, 143, 144, 162, 163, 169, 183
iPhone 15 Pro Max, 5, 8, 12, 16, 23, 24, 29, 34, 143, 169, 183
iPhone 15 series, 16, 64, 144, 154, 156, 159, 169, 175, 177, 179
iPhone 3GS, 18
iPhone camera settings, 20
IPhone Continuity, 181
iPhone filming accessory, 57
iPhone models, 26, 29, 30, 34, 40, 63, 139, 148, 149
IPhone Photos, 150
iPhone Storage, 154, 179
Is it bad that I have so many duplicates?, 139
Is it possible to restore lost images from an iPhone 15?, 98

J

Joby GorillaPod Compact Tripod Stand, 62

K

Keep Burst Mode enabled, 80
Keep the phone near your body., 19

L

Large file sizes, 51
Launch **Frame Grabber**, 22
Launch **iMovie**, 44, 69, 70
Launch **iMovie** from your iPhone., 44
Launch the Camera app, 21, 35, 48, 81, 144, 152, 165, 166, 167, 168, 175, 179
launch the **Camera app.**, 179
Launch the **FaceTime app**, 111, 115, 116
Launch the **FaceTime app.**, 111
launch the **Photos app**, 87, 102, 104, 119, 137, 141
Launch the **Photos app**, 67, 72, 81, 100, 108, 130, 132, 135, 138, 150, 153, 155
Launch the **Settings app.**, 49, 82, 147, 165
Leave a voicemail, 113
LED lights, 57
leverage the device's extensive pixel capabilities, 5
Library, 85, 86, 87, 91, 101, 137
light intensity, 177
Lighting, 32, 147, 178
Live Photo function, 27, 164, 179
Live photos, 22
Live Photos, 13, 14, 16, 27, 80, 91, 118, 179, 180
Locate and open the **Settings app.**, 24
locate the Camera section, 10, 139
Locate the **Grid** and turn it on., 82
Lock the focus and exposure for natural and smooth lighting changes., 21
Log in with your Apple ID, 110
long videos on your iPhone, 94
Low illumination, 161
lower-left corner of the screen, 7
low-light circumstances, 37, 148, 149, 167, 176
low-light settings, 19, 37

M

MACRO PHOTOGRAPHY AND OTHER CAMERA MODES, 143
Mail, 89, 90, 91, 94, 95, 115
Main camera, 29, 182, 183
Maintain the Proper Distance, 178
maintaining a manageable file size, 183
maintaining consistent focus and exposure, 20
Make a FaceTime Call, 111
Make the text curve inwards or outwards, 97
Make use of a tripod stand, 39
Make use of your iPhone's built-in grid, 19
Manually adjust the screen brightness, 105
Manually Creating a Memory on Your iPhone, 123
Max Accessories for Filmmaking, 57
Max features a 5x Telephoto lens, 6
maximum digital zoom of 15x, 6
maximum frame rate, 4, 6, 41
maximum frame rate of 60 frames per second, 4, 6
Media Types, 85, 98, 138
Memoji and Animoji Effects, 114

MEMORY MOVIES, 119
minimizing storage consumption, 5
Minor software issues, 180
Mode Focus Post-Shoot, 65
Moment Blue Flare Anamorphic Lens, 57
Moment Blue Flare Anamorphic Lens for iPhone, 57
Monocular Telescope, 60
Months, 86, 91
Mount your iPhone on a tripod., 21
Move the camera carefully in the direction of the arrow, 21
Moving subjects, 161
Moving the camera closer, 19
Moving the shutter button, 35

N

Navigate to **Settings**, 18, 29, 105, 106, 107, 129
Navigate to the **Camera** section., 49
navigate to the **Settings menu**, 10
New Camera Features, 3
New Camera Features in iPhone 15 Series, 3
Night mode demands a steady hand, 176
Night mode works best, 176

O

Open FaceTime, 111
Open the "**Settings**" app on your iPhone., 154, 157
Open the **FaceTime app**, 114, 117, 118
Open the **Photos app**, 65, 92, 95, 103
Optimize battery charging by turning on and off, 175
Optimized Battery Charging, 175
Organize and delete unwanted photos regularly, 155
overall performance of the device. Moreso, 4
Overhead Stand for your Apple iPhone, 61
Overview, 3, 34, 51, 73, 85, 110, 119, 143, 159

P

painful situation, 169
percent Focus Pixels, 183
Perform a Factory Reset, 160
phone camera lenses, 58
Photographic Styles, 14, 73, 74
PHOTOGRAPHIC STYLES, 73

PHOTOGRAPHIC STYLES, EXPOSURE, AND OTHER CAMERA SETTINGS, 73
photographs or Videos, 89
photography experience, 8, 58
photos and videos, 7, 85, 86, 87, 89, 90, 91, 92, 93, 102, 129, 130, 138, 158, 165, 182
PHOTOS APP, 85
Photos application, 4
Physical buttons, 8
Play the video and pause it, 22
Portrait, 4, 16, 23, 78, 80, 81, 117, 118, 145, 146, 147, 148, 153, 164, 177, 178, 179
portrait mode, 4, 15, 16, 117, 145, 177, 178, 182
Portrait mode, 4, 16, 78, 80, 81, 118, 145, 147, 148, 153, 164, 177, 178, 179
portrait mode feature, 4
portrait mode has undergone a comprehensive overhaul, 4
portrait selfie, 10
portrait shooting, 179
Position the iPhone in the right way, 80
possible impediments., 178
potential hardware diagnostics, 177
power button, 8, 156, 159, 180
practical file size, 183
Prepare Phone Storage, 162
presence of 48MP photographs, 4
Preserve Settings, 144, 159, 162, 178
preserving and sharing images, 183
press the Shutter button one more time, 21
Press the **Shutter button**., 21
Prevent automatic illumination, 20
Prevent automatic illumination changes by locking in exposure, 20
preview monitor by AirPlaying, 20
preview window, 20
previous functionality of earlier versions of iPhones, 4
Privacy and Security, 181, 182
Privacy and Security Site settings, 182
Pro or Pro Max devices., 24
procedures work, 180
Proceed to record a video., 23
process of capturing an image, 8
process of recording a QuickTake video, 11
professional filmmaking endeavors, 57
professional photographers, 58
professional-grade smartphones, 10
ProRAW, 5, 6, 17, 51, 52, 53, 54, 72, 161, 162, 163

ProRAW Max, 17
ProRes 4K recording, 51
ProRes Encoding, 25
ProRes Log option, 25
Protect the Memories Video, 129
Provide Adequate Lighting, 177
provision of 4K video capturing capabilities, 6
purchasing a gimbal, 19

Q

Quickly Convert a Photo, 146
QuickTake, 11, 17, 34, 35, 50, 161, 165
QuickTake mode, 35

R

RAW photo settings, 17
Reboot your iPhone, 177, 180
Receive a FaceTime Call, 112
Recently Deleted, 89, 98, 99, 100, 139
Recents folder, 137
Record a Video, 18
Record a video message, 112
record clear audio, 18
Record HD, 18
Record HD or 4K video, 18
record HDR videos, 4
record high-quality videos., 4
Record in ProRes, 55
Record Professional Videos, 18
Record Video, 18, 29, 31, 37, 38, 49, 55, 112, 113
Record videos with your iPhone camera, 17
recording a gorgeous bike trip, 32
recording a QuickTake video, 34
RECORDING IN PRORAW AND PRORES, 51
recording the video, 28, 64, 65
reduce camera shaking, 32
Reduce the volume of your iPhone, 27
Reduce the volume of your iPhone under the Control Center, 27
reduced frame rate, 40
releasing the volume up and volume down, 180
Remove the Case, 169
Remove the iPhone Cover if Covered, 173
Remove the Object, 63
remove your data, 180

Renaming Photos on iPhone, 141
repair temporary software faults, 177
Requirements, 23
Reset All Settings, 160, 180
Reset Camera Settings, 159, 178
Reset iPhone Settings, 174
resolution and FPS., 55
resolution of 48MP, 17
resolution of standard HEIF images, 5
Rest your elbows on a nearby strong item., 19
Restart Google Chrome, 182
Restart your iPhone, 159, 173
Restoring from Backup, 180
Rode VideoMic, 58, 59
Rode VideoMic Me Compact, 58
Rode VideoMic Me Compact TRRS, 58
Rode VideoMic Me Compact TRRS Cardioid, 58
Rode VideoMic Me Compact TRRS Cardioid Microphone for iPhone, 58
Rode Wireless GO II Compact, 61
Rode Wireless GO II Compact Wireless Mic System, 61
Rotating Photos, 104
running iOS 17, 27, 81, 122

S

Save or share a photo or video you receive, 92
Save Photos to Files, 155
Save to Files, 140, 141, 155
Save to Photos, 141
Save to Quick Notes, 141
Save Video, 68, 69, 121
Schedule Dark Mode to turn on and off automatically, 106
Schedule the Night Shift to turn on and off automatically, 107
screen buttons available, 12
Screen Recording, 71, 72
screen shutter button transforms, 9
Scroll down and choose **Camera**., 41
SDR version, 38
SDR version of the same video, 38
seamless integration, 57, 61, 62
seamless live-streaming, 57
seamless live-streaming processes, 57
Search for Photos, 138
Security or Setting Time Zone, 107

See photo and video information, 86
seizing action-packed, 183
seizing action-packed moments, 183
Select a tilt angle for your picture., 97
Select **Display & Brightness**, 107
Select **Pano mode**., 21
Select the **Video option**., 48
send a video, 94
Send a video using an iCloud link, 94
Send all photo data, 91
Send as iCloud link, 91
sensor-shift optical image stabilization, 3
Set the Focus, 166
Set up your shot using a tripod, 18
setting a new standard for iPhone devices, 183
settings on iPhone, 37
several new privacy features, 102
Shadows, 164, 168
Share, 87, 89, 91, 92, 94, 121, 132, 140, 141, 151, 153, 155
Share photos and videos on iPhone, 89
sharing method, 90, 91
Shoot at a frame rate, 30
Shoot at a frame rate of 24 frames per second, 30
shoot excellent 4K film,, 18
Shoot images, 23
Shoot images in a square ratio, 23
Shoot in bright light, 42
shoot in Log mode, 23
Shooting slow motion using an iPhone camera, 40
Silvertone, 82
simplicity of the iPhone's built-in time-lapse, 39
simplicity of the iPhone's built-in time-lapse capability, 39
slide to power off, 180
Slo-mo, 23, 40, 41, 42, 43, 45, 46, 144
SmallRig Video Cage for iPhone, 57
smartphone photography, 97
Smudges on the lens, 161
Sony Folding Professional Closed Ear Headphones, 59
sophisticated controls and settings, 179
Speak with Apple Support, 177
Speaking of time-lapse films, 21
stabilization function, 32
Stable Support, 176
stable video footage., 32
start a FaceTime call, 111, 118

Start your iPhone again., 175
Stickers and Filters, 114
still/live images and movies., 163
storage capacity, 5, 6, 51, 169
Storage is an issue, 169
Sufficient iPhone Battery, 39
super-high-resolution, 4, 5, 183
super-high-resolution option, 183
superior audio quality, 61
superior low-light performance, 4
support video capture, 16
swift and accurate focusing, 183

T

Take a Burst, 163
Take a Live Photo in FaceTime on an iPhone, 118
Take a panoramic photo of a landscape, 23
Take a photo, 17, 175
Take Multiple Photos, 176
Take panoramic photos with your iPhone camera, 21
Take RAW pictures, 53
Take Several Shots, 179
Take still photos and Live photos in Photo mode., 22
Tap **Camera** in the Settings app., 52, 54
Tap the **Overflow symbol**, 102
Tap the playhead, 70
Tap the **Select button**, 88, 103
tap the **shutter symbol**, 56
tele lens, 12
Telephoto camera, 183
the AE/AF Lock indication, 32
the Apple ProRes option, 24, 25
The Arkon Pro Phone, 61
The Arkon Pro Phone or Camera Stand, 61
The Arkon Pro Stand, 62
The Arkon Pro Stand boasts, 62
The benefit of Live Text?, 150
the camera app, 3, 8, 11, 13, 14, 17, 26, 27, 33, 34, 149, 158, 159, 160, 163, 170, 173
The Camera app, 4, 16
the Camera app., 7, 25, 52, 73, 75, 78, 176, 178
the Camera application, 7, 8, 15, 17, 173
the camera application interface, 13
the Camera app's toolbar, 179
The camera captures video, 37
The Control Center, 27
the default mode, 5, 22

The depth-sensing technology, 178
the depth-sensing technology., 178
The device also offers an Action mode, 6
The device boasts, 183
the dual camera setup, 4
The enhanced zoom capabilities, 6
The entire iPhone 15 Pro lineups, 6
the exposure/focus lock option, 20
the Formats option, 24
The iOS Photos app's Markup function, 95
The iPhone 15 Pro, 5, 6, 12, 23, 161, 183
the iPhone 15 Pro Max, 12, 183
the iPhone 15 Pro Max showcases, 183
the iPhone 15 Series, 3, 26, 27, 33, 34, 37, 74, 77, 85, 116, 149
The iPhone 15 Series, 20
The iPhone dual-camera system, 183
The iPhone Photos app, 46
The latest iPhones, 19
the lighting conditions, 32, 75
The macro mode, 14, 15
The maximum duration, 56
The Most Common Causes of Blurry Photos and Videos, 161
the new features and functions, 3
the **Night mode icon**, 176
The People's Album, 123
The photo's resolution, 22
the **'Play Memory Movie'** option, 124
the previous model, 3
the Pro Max result, 6
the Pro Max result in a 5x optical zoom, 6
The Pro model features, 6
The Pro model features a telephoto lens, 6
The Pro series features, 183
The procedures for forcibly restarting your iPhone 15, 180
The QuickTake feature, 11
the Save Image option, 22
the top-right corner of the screen, 65, 125, 157
the ultrawide camera, 47
the USB-C connection, 16, 93
The use of RAW format, 17
The utilization of ProRAW, 5
the volume up button, 10, 35
Time-lapse, 20, 23, 35, 37, 39, 144
time-lapse video, 34, 35, 50
Tips for Better Night Photography, 149

Tips for Using the Timer on an iPhone to Take Photos, 79
Toggle Low Power Mode on and off, 174
Trimming a Video in the Photos App, 67
Trimming an iPhone video for Instagram, 69
Troubleshooting For Sharper Photos, 165
TROUBLESHOOTING ISSUES, 159
Turn Dark Mode on or off, 105
Turn Lock Camera on and off, 38
Turn off the iPhone., 170
Turn on and off Enhanced Stabilization, 38
Turn on and off the stereo recording, 38
Turn on FaceTime, 110
Turn on Silent Mode, 26
Turn on the Grid, 31
Turn the Camera flash ON and then OFF, 173
Turn the Night Shift on or off, 107
Turn True Tone on or off, 107

U

unattractive pixelation, 19
underlying software issues, 180
Unnecessary Photo, 136
unprecedented optical zoom capability, 183
Unsteady hands, 161
Update iOS, 159, 180
upgraded 24MP mode, 17
USB 3 technology, 6
Use a Flash, 176
Use a tripod, 79, 149, 168, 178
Use a tripod or other kind of stabilization, 178
Use a VPN for Additional Security, 156
Use Apple Watch as a preview window, 20
Use iCloud Photos, 154
Use Live Photo, 164
Use Macro Control, 162
Use My Photo Stream, 155
Use Night Mode, 167
use of the volume-up button, 10
Use Password Security and Biometrics, 156
Use Shutter Button, 163
use the Camera app to capture videos, 17
use the Camera app to capture videos and QuickTake videos., 17
Use the iPhone's several shooting modes, 20
use the Perfect App from the App Store, 39
Use the rear camera lenses to shoot, 19

Use Third-Party Apps, 179
Use third-party cloud services, 155
use your Memoji in a variety of ways, 114
using a microfiber cloth, 177
Using Apple's Photos app, 95
using applications, 6
Using Phonto, 96
Using the Rule of Thirds in Your iPhone Photos, 83
using the selfie camera., 19
using the slider, 76, 176
using third-party camera applications, 179

V

variety of purposes, 47
variety of styles, 96
various camera modes, 13
Vibrance, 164
Vibrant, 73, 74, 81
vibrant color reproduction, 4
Video on iPhone 15 Pro, 16
video published as an Instagram Post, 69
video recording, 9, 11, 13, 16, 18, 29, 34, 35, 37, 50, 62
VIDEO RECORDING, 34
Video Stabilization, 165
videographers, 58
video's resolution, 22
View individual images, 86
View outside Frame, 31
View photos and videos in the Photos app on the iPhone, 85
Vivid Cool, 82
Vivid Warm, 81
vloggers, 57, 61

vloggers and creators, 57
volume down button, 10
volume down buttons, 8, 180

W

well-suited for capturing close-up shots, 183
What exactly are iPhone Memories?, 119
What exactly are Macro Photos?, 143
What exactly are photographic styles?, 73
What Is the Difference Between an iPhone Folder and a Photo Album?, 130
What is the speed of an iPhone slow-motion video?, 40
Which iPhones are capable of macro photography?, 143
Which iPhones have night mode?, 149
While recording videos, take photos or screenshots, 28
While the music is playing, take photos or screenshots, 28
white balance, 33, 38, 51, 77, 162
White Balance, 33, 38
Why are photographic styles so appealing?, 73
wider variety, 31
wider variety of tonal nuances, 31
wildlife photography, 183
wireless microphones, 61

Z

Zoom In, 142
Zoom levels on iPhone 15 Pro, 12
Zoom Out, 141

Printed in Great Britain
by Amazon

40787162R00117